Children Composi

Composing is part of the mainstream music curriculum for many children yet children's music does not receive the same attention as their art or creative writing. *Children Composing 4–14* traces the ways in which composing can be organised and taught within the school music curriculum, drawing on children's own music-making activities. This practical book looks at how teaching composing can enable children to progress by acquiring musical skills and understanding, while developing their own sense of musical purpose. One of the main concerns of the book is the need to sustain continuity and quality in children's composing experience as they move through each phase of music education.

Children's composing is considered in relation to the wider musical context in which they grow up, including cultural differences in composing roles and in perceptions of composing and composers. Projects that bring children into contact with professional composers are critically examined, and suggestions are made for ways of ensuring that composing in schools is rooted in the musical world outside. *Children Composing 4–14* is intended for teachers of music in primary and secondary schools, composers who work in education, parents, carers and youth leaders with an interest in children's music.

Joanna Glover is Subject Leader for Music Education at Bath Spa University College, where she teaches on courses in initial and inservice education, and undergraduate and postgraduate music programmes. Her previous publications include *Music in the Early Years* and *Primary Music: Later Years*, both co-authored with Susan Young and published by RoutledgeFalmer.

Children Composing 4–14

Joanna Glover

London and New York

First published 2000 by RoutledgeFalmer
11 New Fetter Lane, London EC4P 4EE

Simultaneously published in the USA and Canada
by RoutledgeFalmer
29 West 35th Street, New York, NY 10001
RoutledgeFalmer is an imprint of the Taylor & Francis Group

© 2000 Joanna Glover

Typeset in Goudy by
Curran Publishing Services Ltd, Norwich
Printed and bound in Great Britain by St Edmundsbury Press,
Bury St. Edmunds, Suffolk.

British Library Cataloguing in Publication Data
A catalogue record for this book is available from the British Library

Library of Congress Cataloging in Publication Data
Glover, Joanna.
    Children composing, 4–14 / Joanna Glover.
        p. cm
    Includes bibliographical references (p.) and index.
        1. School music – Instruction and study. 2. Composition (Music)
I. Title: Children composing, four to fourteen. II. Title.

    MT155 .G56 2000
    372.87'4–dc21
                                                                00-042192
ISBN 0–415–23073–X (pbk)
ISBN 0–415–23072–1 (hbk)

Contents

This book has a companion website: www.bathspa.ac.uk/children-composing/

Figures

Acknowledgements

My sincerest thanks go to all the children, teachers, colleagues and friends who have helped me, wittingly or unwittingly, in the writing of this book.

I am particularly grateful to Pam Burnard, Philip Cashian, Marie Coombes, Lesley Flash, Linda Fursland, Deirdre Gribbin, Fiona Hunt, Brian Loane, Hugh Nankivell and Susan Young for their contributions and support, and to Chew Stoke CEVA Primary School and St.Mary's CEVA Primary School, Thornbury. Finally I would like to record special thanks to Stephen and Heather Ward for their invaluable help, particularly during the final stages of the book.

Music copyist: Janet Lunt
Website designed by: Judy Hardy

Note on the drawings

Children make their own music from the earliest age. From experiences in school and beyond they build their own concepts of what composing involves. In fact, though, children's ideas of composers are often somewhat fragile, as the descriptions on pages 114–15 suggest: 'they'd have loads of paper all over the floor . . . probably quite messy . . . someone with grey hair . . . they're 60 or 70 because they have to get used to writing music first'. These drawings show how the concept of composing becomes bound up with images of keyboards, writing and notation, with the interesting addition of a computer (Figure 2). Accessing such perceptions can enable teachers to help children widen their understanding of what composing can be like for themselves and others.

Figure 1: 'A composer', by Victoria Davey, aged 8

Figure 2: 'A composer', by Ben Waldock, aged 7 years and 11 months

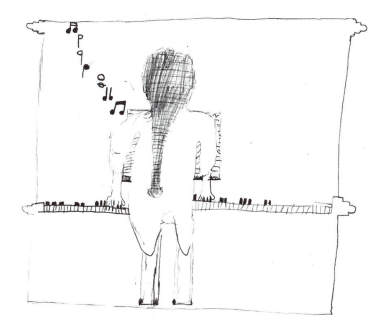

Figure 3: 'A composer', by Max Oakley, aged 8

Figure 4: 'A composer', by Anna Riddiford, aged 7 and a half

Chapter 1

Children's music

I made up a tune, because me and my brother sing tunes in the bath. So I was trying to think of one up because I've never made a really *good* one. So I did and now we sing it over and over again until someone says: 'Stop!'

I made some music on my little computer. I pressed some keys and then I've got a little button that says Play. I pressed it and it plays my music.

'My name is Paul.' 'My name is Hilman.' 'My name is Ashley.' 'We are The Three Beaters.'

Children are inventive and capable as music makers. They make music independently of being shown or taught how to do so. For very young children, this music is often intrinsic to other activity, as part of play, movement or the ordinary round of daily life. They improvise songs spontaneously as early as they acquire language. Left to play with instruments, they meticulously investigate the sound world offered and go on to pattern and order sounds into musical shape.

Through the early primary years, children compose songs and instrumental music, alone and with others, given no more than opportunity, time and freedom from interruption. Later, children learning instruments extend their practising into creating music of their own, limited only by their skills in producing and controlling the sound. Such pieces often exceed, in both technical and musical demands, the boundaries of the repertoire they are given to play by teachers. Those with access to keyboards and computers compose music that takes advantage of the rich sound palette available and the technological facility to layer, save and edit their music, creating it in stages. As their proficiency with language increases, children write songs as easily as stories and poems, showing themselves more than capable of finding the tunes and accompaniments to carry words expressively. Pre-adolescents form musical partnerships and small groups, composing their own song material and rehearsing it assiduously, often adding dance or instrumental backing.

As children move into adolescence, the factors inhibiting this self-driven compositional development are mainly those arising from an acute awareness of the sound of the children's music in relation to the music they hear around them. This is particularly so if performance skills and technical understanding are lacking. Even so, many continue to be motivated enough to generate their own music, particularly if there are facilities at hand for seeing it through to performance or recording. In the field of popular music they learn techniques from each other and through repeated listening and imitation.

Through all this, children's energy and imagination, and something magnetic about the power of musical sound, drive a creativity that draws on the musical worlds which have surrounded them since birth. They find purposes for composing that reflect both their inner sense of music's possibilities and the ways in which music is woven expressively and functionally into community life. Their composing has musical intention and cultural currency. And, for many, it takes place largely independently of schools or teachers.

Room has been made for composing in schools as part of the music curriculum, in principle at least. Paradoxically, however, it does not always follow that the composing activities children are given acknowledge, support or build on the kind of self-reliant music-making they are capable of. One of the reasons for this is that we, as adult members of the wider community, have only a rather vague sense of children's music-making capabilities. There is surprisingly little clarity as to what children's own music sounds like, what can be expected of children as composers, or how composing in school might connect to the musical worlds beyond.

The musical creativity children bring to composing is too vital to remain unheard. It is important for each child to know their own musical 'voice' and to have the skill and confidence to develop it. It is also important that the adult community and those in educational settings recognise this. Children's independent compositional abilities are too easily undermined when music education places value on performing and listening at the expense of improvising and composing. This is the musical equivalent of teaching reading and listening but leaving out speaking and writing. If the liveliness and complexity of very young children's music-making can be sustained and built on skilfully through the years of primary schooling and on into adolescence, each person can take into adulthood an undamaged and enduring sense of musical self and self-respect.

The aim of this book is to give an account of children's composing, from 4 to 14, which may help teachers bring together the dual considerations of encouraging children's musical and compositional development and helping them to integrate work done in school with the musical worlds they experience beyond. The intention is to explore how children's own music-making activity can be built on through the ways in which teachers and composers work with pupils in school. There is a need to clarify ways in which the overall planning for this aspect of the music curriculum can be properly grounded in an understanding of how children as composers grow up.

Many of the pioneers of children's composing, from early twentieth century teachers such as Satis Coleman to much later composer educators – Maxwell Davies, Paynter or Schafer, for example – have had very clear ideas of how pupils' composing relates to the wider musical world. By contrast, recent curriculum planners at every level have been remarkably silent on this point, and have perhaps even viewed it as non-problematic. As a consequence, the way composing is planned for pupils can become a rather random patchwork of experiences. Some of these may be rich samples in themselves, but when tacked together they lack coherence with pupils' musical experience beyond school. More serious still is the lack in curriculum planning of any sense of the inner creativity of each child as the energy which drives their music-making development. Although there is a growing body of research on different aspects of children's musical and compositional development and processes, little sense of this has filtered through to curriculum approaches, particularly for younger pupils.

It is not enough to adopt composing as part of a music curriculum and then specify a selection of curriculum activities. Curriculum planning must be driven by a vision of children's composing as it relates to their individual creativity and developing capabilities and as it finds its place in relation to the adult worlds of music and music-making. There is much excellent work being done by teachers in primary and secondary schools and by composers working with children through composer-in-education projects. While positive experiences are never lost, it is still the case that some of the potential benefits of this work become diluted in terms of pupils' longer term development by a lack of continuity and coherence. Students in secondary school are heard covering the same ground introduced five years ago in primary school and accomplishing less. Revisiting areas of work with new skills and experience is valuable in deepening understanding, but often the reality is based on low expectations and a loss of direction because no-one is quite sure how compositional development goes.

Alongside the development of children's music in schools, the concept of composing has itself been opening up. Unparalleled global evolution in cross-cultural perceptions of music have resulted in populations whose musical culture is more complex in mix, fusion and access to different world musics than ever before. In such a climate, any fixed notion of what composing *is* has been thoroughly deconstructed as it becomes clear that the processes of making music are as diverse as the musics themselves. 'Composing' cannot any more be seen as one thing. Unless this is acknowledged, the pluralism of contemporary music sits uneasily alongside a curriculum built to ignore it. The culture of western classical music in which the notion of the individual composer was most dominant in western education systems, that of western classical music, is now regaining its proportions alongside other musical genres in which the idea of the composer is different, sometimes radically so, or non-existent. Just as children's composing becomes something widespread within our education systems, there is a real sense in which we, as community members, can no longer have any simple picture of what composing is.

In order to centre composing activities in school on pupils' needs, and to avoid vastly underestimating what they are capable of, teachers have to listen to the music children make independently. Only by making contact with children's musical thinking and imagination as it comes through their own improvising and composing, and taking this seriously, can the details of planning for composing as part of the class and school curriculum take shape. Once the connection is made, composing can take off, for individuals and the class, in a way that increases skills and understanding and that stimulates, instead of sidelining, individual imagination, musical purposes and response.

A central question for this book is: what does children's music *sound* like? There is no single answer to this, of course, nor would we expect there to be. But it raises the issue of how much, or how little, we have been able to hear children's music and value it as music in its own right. How far does children's improvised or composed music take its place in the musical life of the community, not through the odd isolated presentation, or through images of prodigies viewed somewhat as circus acts, but as part of an integrated and organic whole? The measure of the quality of composing in music education must be connected to the ways in which children can contribute within the wider musical world.

At a more practical level, this book shares the issue facing any book about children's music: that of how to make the music itself heard and exchangeable. To this end, the book has a companion website (www.bathspa.ac.uk/childre-composing) which offers examples of children's work and a forum for ongoing discussion and contributions. Within the book itself, examples have been kept to a minimum and are largely focused on the early stages of emergent musical ideas. The website is based on the optimistic assumption that, one way or another, readers can gain internet access to the music in a form which can perhaps avoid the rather museum-like qualities of written examples or a once-only CD accompanying the book. Others may find the website first and thereby find their way to this book. The fact that there is no easy solution to making the music available underlines one of the central themes of the book. In the end there is no better way to explore children's music than to stand back, observe, and listen to the stream of musical invention so readily forthcoming from the children with whom we live and work.

What does children's music *sound* like?

As a young teacher in the 1970s, I had most of my conversations about children's composition work in music with art teachers: painters, potters, sculptors and designers. They were used to looking critically at pupils' work. Art making, as opposed to art appreciation, had been central to art education all along. In the fields of children's painting and drawing at least, there were well-established understandings of developmental patterns and stages of experience, and there was a history of ongoing research investigating these. There was also a recognition of issues facing teachers working with children's art, such as how to handle the relationship between skill acquisition and creativity or how to support students through the crises encountered by many young artists when vision persistently exceeds the technique or capacity to realise it. Above all though, there was a familiarity with the whole range and scope of the art that pupils might produce, from the youngest pre-schoolers right through to those who specialise and go on to art school foundation courses. Against this common understanding there was also an eye for the unexpected, the unusual, the work with special qualities of its own which might stand out amongst the rest.

Many of my generation of music teachers were working with composition as a mainstream area of classroom music, in primary and secondary schools. Yet, despite the fact that there had been pockets of quite extensive work in composition long before our time, we were doing so largely against a background of silence. Not silence in the classroom, far from it. But there was an almost complete absence of shared experience among music educators, or parents, or the wider community, of what the music children make for themselves sounds like, and hence of what can be expected when they compose.

Composing is now part of the mainstream music curriculum for children in schools in many parts of the world. Approaches to this differ and so does the extent to which government or state guidelines ensure that all children have continuing experience of composing through primary or elementary and secondary schooling. One way and another, however, children's own music-making has found its way onto the main agenda. Music which is made by pupils themselves is established as part of what is to be expected within the scope of 'school music' across a wide range of educational contexts. Despite all this activity, there is still a noticeable absence of general recognition and understanding of the music children produce. For many people, including plenty of those embarking on teaching composition as part of the music curriculum, this is still uncharted territory; and in the public domain, children's music – in the sense of music made up by children – is only just audible. For many, the questions remain: what does children's music sound like? And what can be expected when children compose?

There is, of course, something odd about having to ask these questions at all. If there is such a thing as 'children's music' – music that is genuinely children's own – why would we not as a community be already familiar with it, or even remember something of the music we once made as children ourselves? Children's art making is recognised at some level by most people, if only in the form of pictures drawn and offered as gifts. Their art is visible to anyone, in forms ranging from home and playgroup displays to impressive art shows on school open days, in public libraries or galleries, and right across the age range.

In the field of art, this public recognition is not a recent development by any means. An *Exhibition of Children's Drawings* was held at the artist Roger Fry's Omega Workshops in London in 1917. 'The Omega exhibition was a milestone in art education, being the first time in Britain that children's art was exhibited in its own right and for its own qualities' (Holdsworth 1988).

The artist and teacher Marion Richardson visited this exhibition and received encouragement from Fry for her own work with children, examples of which were included in the Omega collection. Two decades later, in 1938,

Richardson's *Exhibition of Children's Art* at County Hall, London was another such key event, movingly described in her book, *Art and the Child* (1948). This was a culmination of years of pioneering work by Richardson with her own pupils in Dudley and later with teachers and colleagues such as Reginald Tomlinson during her years as Inspector of Art for the London County Council. Her influence was profoundly important in shifting the emphasis in art teaching away from approaches of pure copying and exercises towards the cultivation of children's own imagination and vision. In 1939, Lowenfeld published *The Nature of Creative Activity*, giving an experimental psychologist's perspective on children's drawings in a study of the visual and non-visual sources of creative imagination. Herbert Read's *Education through Art* (1943) offered an extensive exploration of children's imagination through art making within a theoretical framework based in psychology and education. In 1947, the year after Richardson's death, Alexander Barclay-Russell inaugurated a *National Exhibition of Children's Art* at the Whitechapel Art Gallery under the auspices of the London County Council. This continued as an annual event, touring internationally, with sponsorship from Cadbury's among others. The 'Child Art' movement has a long and substantial history in Britain and has played a major part in changing perceptions not just of teachers, but of parents and the community generally.

Where are the musical equivalents of these public acknowledgements of children's art as something worth making available to audiences beyond the classroom? In youth music festivals, platforms for hearing children's compositions have begun to be included but are nowhere near as well established as those for performance of the music of others. Pupils' compositions increasingly appear on school concert programmes but still as a relatively small proportion of the music presented. Repertoire for instrumental lessons, school music groups, county youth bands and orchestras rarely includes pupils' compositions and there are still few county or national music events for composers comparable to the enormous range of opportunities for young performers.

The ongoing development of pedagogy and the study of children's art itself have also been reflected in the training of art teachers. At the Leeds School of Art, for example, courses for intending art teachers seem to have had some child-centred perspective from at least as early as 1914 when theoretical instruction included *Mind Training – The Mind of the Student*. The art teaching diploma course during the 1940s and 1950s included lectures giving insight into, among other things, *The Characteristics of Children's Drawings* (Milton Smith 1985). A parallel might be drawn with children's creative writing. David Holbrook's classic book *Children's Writing*, published in 1967, was intended as a handbook for student teachers, a sampler for the study of children's creative writing. The approach to the teaching of English which Holbrook recommends 'begins with our experience of children and their writing, and moves from there towards work in literature'.

If they (student teachers) work by creative methods, they will begin to collect examples of children's work. They will learn to study and evaluate children's writing, and they can bring samples back to college, for discussion. . . . [T]he study and discussion of children's creative expression is if anything more exacting than normal literary criticism and so requires a special training.

Holbrook (1967a: preface)

This anthology, in conjunction with the book it accompanies, *The Exploring Word* (Holbrook 1967), not only takes seriously the writing children produce as of value in itself, but expects teachers to become skilled at understanding and assessing pupils' work. Furthermore, children's writing is seen as the window onto their 'poetic needs', enabling teachers to make links with literature which will match pupils' interests with material selected for study. The approach of the English National Writing Project built on a sustained tradition of 'finding out what children are able to write rather than what they cannot write' (Czerniewska 1988). How many courses for intending teachers even today include serious study of the music children produce? Without some fundamental grounding in listening to children's composition, it is not surprising when teachers feel at sea about what to expect or how to handle children's work.

In the past, there have been good reasons why children's music was harder to catch, collect and display than children's art or writing. Time-based arts are by their nature elusive. They require performers to realise the pieces, and the business of seeing composed music through to performance depends either on the presence of the composer as performer, or on processes of notation or some alternative form of communication enabling others to recreate the music. The alternative approach, that of recording and saving the music, has become almost universally available, but during the earlier twentieth century, when the interest in child art was rapidly taking off, recording techniques for music were relatively specialist. Heinz Werner, who in 1917 (the same year as the Omega exhibition) published a report of his research into very young children's songs, based his work on recordings collated on phonographic plates. These appear to be the first acoustical documentation of children's songs (Sundin 1998). The Pillsbury Foundation Studies (see Chapter 4), a research project into young children's music carried out in California between 1937 and 1948, included more than 2,000 recordings of the children's activities made with a mechanical disc recording machine, from which many transcriptions were made (Wilson 1981). It is easy to see how in the past children's music has been less easy to bring to any audience beyond the very immediate. For half a century, however, rapidly progressing technologies of audio recording, radio, video and TV, computers and the Internet, as well as greater opportunities for children to perform live in a range of venues have all become readily available. The difficulties of capturing children's music by recording or making it available to wider audiences do not entirely explain why the broader recognition of children's ability to make music, as well as to perform it, has lagged so far behind the other arts.

Neither can this be accounted for by an absence of pioneering work by individual educators. The growing interest in children's art through the first half of the twentieth century and beyond certainly had parallels in music education. For example, from the 1920s in New York, Satis Coleman was developing an approach to early years music education based on the fundamental principle of the priority of the child's need for musical experiences on which knowledge can later be built (Southcott 1990). The experiences Dr Coleman sought to provide included singing, based on a repertoire which included children's own composed songs alongside traditional and folk songs, improvising vocal conversations, individual instrument-making and exploring, improvising and composing with a wide range of simple instruments, playing in ensembles, rhythm games and also dance and movement. She used the term 'creative music' in her writings (Coleman 1922) and placed considerable value on children's musical invention, developing in addition a simplified notation system by which to record their melodies. She was concerned that children's composing should not be delayed by expecting them to learn to notate music first. As an educator, a writer for teachers and parents, and a practitioner, Coleman continued to develop her pioneering approaches into the 1950s.

More idiosyncratically, the composer Walford Davies, working for the Gramophone Company, introduced the composing of melodies into his teaching lectures for schools, recorded on double-sided records in 1922. 'Pupils were provided with an ABC of tune building: Adventure, Balance and Completion' (Cox 1997). However, examples of tunes composed by elementary school pupils were included on a supplementary record and this continued to be an intrinsic part of the musical expectations of pupils in his BBC school broadcasts from 1924. Contributions from children in schools were included in the pamphlets and in the broadcasts themselves. Most interesting from the current perspective is the tension between Walford Davies' implicit endorsement of children's abilities to compose melodies, and the explicit disclaimer from the Gramophone Company's magazine:

> We should like to clear up a misunderstanding that seems to have got abroad. Dr Davies has no intention or wish of making us all composers. He uses the composition method as a means for us to obtain a grasp of the art of music, whereby we shall be able to proceed to acquire a full understanding of all the music there is in the world.
>
> The Voice 1922 (cited in Cox 1997)

Such ambivalence, between on the one hand the desire to widen musical access and recognise children's musical capabilities and, on the other, wanting to reserve the notion of composing as applicable only to a hallowed few, still surfaces today. This goes some way towards accounting for why so relatively little value has been placed on children's composing, either as a worthwhile activity in itself or as producing music of intrinsic value and interest. Even during more recent decades, when a considerable amount of composing has gone on in schools, it has been by no means unusual in the UK for specialist music teachers, instrumental teachers and even their pupils, to regard children's composing as not really 'proper music'. It is still exceptional rather than a norm for entry requirements for higher education music courses to include composition folios with recordings, or to allow these to balance or replace instrumental performance. Yet within British national curricula guidelines, all pupils have been composing music up to the age of 14; and this extends to16 if they have taken Music GCSE (General Certificate of Secondary Education). These attitudes both display and reinforce the lack of valuing of young composers' work, while at the same time curriculum activity is promoting it. They are extraordinary, whether viewed from the perspectives of the classical music world's prioritising of composers above performers (Cook 1998), or of the employment demands for composers in the music industries. In order to understand why children's composing is treated with such ambivalence in education and has such a fragile presence beyond, other factors have to be considered. Why are we as a community so unfamiliar with what children's music sounds like?

Chapter 2

Children and composing

Today, the cultural surroundings in which many children grow up are likely to be complex in terms of the multiple musical styles and influences encountered, whether in their immediate surroundings at home, or through the media and beyond. If it is to make sense culturally, children's music-making has somehow to be seen in relation to this wider context, with all its variety and richness. The most central models of adult composers offered in schools are those of western classical music. Although these represent only one part of the much wider musical picture of children's lives, as models in education they can occupy disproportionate space. More than that, they offer the 'prototype' of what a composer is and does. And these composers do not belong to a musical culture in which everyone makes their own music. On the contrary, the idea is promoted that they are a rare species set apart, exceptional geniuses, with gifts and inspiration beyond those to which any ordinary person can aspire. This is a very specific historical legacy of western nineteenth-century romanticism and the music historians who followed and enhanced this mythology. But it still holds immense power and overshadows children's music learning in many ways. The consequence is that, even in school, there is a conflict between the idea of endorsing the capabilities of all children to make their own music, and what is represented by the composers who have become, even by default, the prevalent models for this. Somewhere along the line the frame of reference shifts from the ordinary expectations of every pupil to the legacy (and they are mostly dead) of a few composers within the particular genres and styles of classical music. This presents composition as focused on the few with an assumption that most cannot do it. It also presents a model of composing which does not transfer easily into how composers work in other musical fields, such as popular, film or traditional music. This creates a tension between children's experience of music in school and beyond.

An even greater conflict is with the musical practice of the adult population. There is good reason to believe that everyone can compose, but not everyone does. Indeed many would not even consider trying. And the considerable wealth of 'ordinary' people's composing activity is often well disguised by being described in other ways: 'I only write songs for myself', 'we do some of our own material alongside the cover stuff'. Or it may be seen as purely functional within its immediate context and therefore in some way not 'counting'. The latter, which might include, for example, composing hymns, gospel songs and anthems for the church choir, may take place on an amateur basis, but is often essentially no different in context from the purely functional music written by many 'Great Composers'. The difficulty in all this is that, from both adults' and children's perspectives it can become hard to see what in the adult world children's composing relates to. The view might be taken that either this is just children playing childishly at something they will never really practise as adults, or that there must be some strange revolution going on in which suddenly all will become Composers, with a capital C.

Arguably, there has been a revolution going on, but the revolution is in adult perceptions and not in what children do, have always done and are capable of doing in making their own music. The change in perception centres on taking account of all the music-making across the whole community, adults and children, and in valuing creative musical work, whoever is doing it. Once such work becomes visible and audible, professional composing takes its place as a part only of the much wider field of all musical creativity. This in turn opens up the opportunity for relating children's composing to the work of professionals, present or past, on a freer and more healthy basis. There are exceptionally 'gifted' musicians within any time or any musical culture whose vision, imagination and powers of communication take us into new worlds of experience. But if there is no free flow of musical energy across the community at large, everyone's music is diminished. This is why it is important to hear children's work and to become familiar with it as a valid part of all composed music. For the music is there already and the challenge is to sustain rather than to curtail its development into maturity. This needs to happen in a climate which is consonant with the breadth of music children experience and in which the musicality of everyone, adult or child is endorsed.

In an interview about his music, the British composer Maxwell Davies talks about his work with pupils at Cirencester Grammar School in the early 1960s.

> And being a composer, I wrote pieces for the school choir and the school orchestra, a junior orchestra, for school plays, whatever. But also encouraged the kids to compose. And I was very impressed by the lack of inhibition of their composition, particularly when dealing with theatre pieces. Theatre pieces which they composed in groups and made simple tunes and sound effects and dance numbers or whatever. The boys and girls experienced these things as a part of normal classwork, and I had them write their own music down properly, and rehearse it and perform it, and as individuals many made their contribution to the music for a school play or whatever. Their lack of inhibition I thought very, very interesting . . . watching these kids compose, I realised that they were getting wonderful musical images which I was not getting; and that gave me . . . *envy*, if you like!
>
> (Dufallo 1989)

Here the partnership runs both ways. A teacher who is a practising composer is able to model what it is to be a composer, writing music for any situation or group of musicians as the need arises. And the children witness this and are involved in performing music written directly for them. In turn, they are encouraged to do the same, are shown the processes and their music is valued, not just as schoolwork but by the teacher's own interest from a composer's point of view. In this way the musical energy flows between the two.

Although a range of classroom activities have been developed which cluster under the general description of composing, there seems little consensus in curriculum planning about what composing means either for young children or for the population at large, as an ordinary activity in which any and all of us can participate. Without a frame of reference that is wide-ranging and linked to real musical experiences in the musical worlds outside school, the development of composing skills and a sense of musical empowerment has little chance to flourish. Most of us have an idea of the range of creative language use that threads through people's lives: story and joke telling, diary keeping, poetry writing and more sustained biographies, family histories, novel or play-writing. We see how this can develop from children's earliest language play, rhyme and story making and imaginative dialogues and dramatisations. But how and where does the stream of musical invention which can be heard in the pre-school nursery transform into the wide range of activities that constitute adult music-making, amateur and professional? At what point do we begin to view, or hear, children's work as composing?

Paynter and Aston articulate very clearly the relationship they see between children's creative work and that of professional artists. Their book *Sound and Silence*, which introduced a series of projects exploring compositional materials and techniques, became a seminal contribution to the development of children's work in composition in British schools and beyond.

> Artists of all kinds function as visionaries and commentators: their job is not simply to entertain us. We rely upon them to help us come to terms with life and its problems. The art that is *most* relevant to us is that of our own time. We need the professional artist but at the same time we must also cultivate the artist within ourselves, for each one of us has something of that child-like innocence which is the characteristic of the artistic mind, which draws fresh inspiration from familiar things and expresses feelings in words, action, visual symbols or music. We must not stifle this innocent eye or ear; our understanding of the professional artists' work may depend considerably on our ability to participate, even a little, in their activities.
>
> (Paynter and Aston 1970: 4)

As composers and educators, Paynter and Aston endorse the creative potential in all of us, and in all children. Developing this musically is seen as something to be valued in its own right as part of a broad, liberal education for each individual. It is an endeavour in which the relationship between children's work and the creativity of professional composers, particularly contemporary composers, is seen as playing an intrinsic role. What is shared in this is the contemporary experience: 'The musical techniques of our time are relevant to our situation because they grow from it'. The range of contemporary musical style on which the *Sound and Silence* projects draw is wide. Although contemporary 'classical' composers predominate, the work reaches beyond into traditional and popular music. It also includes examples of children's music both in the text and for listening to. On all counts this was groundbreaking work in music education and a catalyst for a new era in children's composition.

Today, it is in making the connections between children's composing and the rest that the teaching ground shifts uneasily, and it should do. It is no longer possible to approach composing in education with anything other than a pluralist view of what composing music encompasses. There is good classroom practice developing composing across different musical styles and music-making approaches, but it is not always accompanied by clarity in acknowledging these differences, either with pupils or in curriculum planning. National guidelines and resource materials tend to present composing as if it were a straightforward, culturally neutral activity. The distinctions between different composing processes belonging to different musical styles and genres are rarely made explicit for pupils or taken account of in practice. Yet, as the musical territory offered for exploration moves between traditional, folk, art or popular idioms, the composing role shifts. As musical investigations draw on different world traditions, the composing practices which belong to these are revealed as very different, or the composer simply vanishes. Musics in which it is the performers' creativity through improvisation within given frameworks or practices that lies at the heart of new invention and expression are often given a relatively low profile in schools. These hold a crucial perspective on the making of music, showing how the role of the performer too is contingent on a particular set of cultural practices. Finally, information technology has brought a whole new raft of possibilities for generating and processing musical sound, setting composing into another, quite different, relationship with performance and performing skills. Working with children composing entails explicit exploration of these different roles, if it is to make musical sense in a pluralist world.

The consequence of not clarifying this multiplicity, and the tensions in how school music-making relates, or fails to relate, to music beyond, is that the cost is paid in the lack of development and progression in pupils' learning. If composing in school is always a one-off activity, linked randomly to different topics beneath which lie fundamentally different composing practices, there is never an opportunity for a child's work to find roots and grow healthily without being repeatedly torn up and moved somewhere else. This is another way in which children's music can become fragmented and submerged.

Composing in the curriculum

In primary schools, composing made its way into the mainstream curriculum in the wake of the creative developments in other arts, most notably art and creative writing. Since it was the norm for a primary class teacher to teach the whole curriculum – although not always including music, it must be said – there was a logical extension to be made in applying to music creative approaches that were already in use in other subjects. Furthermore, many of these teachers were seeing at first hand the quality of the work children could produce in art and language, so that the comparison with music became all the more forceful. Additional encouragement for children's own musical invention came with the development in schools from the 1930s of Carl Orff's Schulwerk, through which instrumental and vocal improvisation were fostered, albeit within fairly tight parameters. By the mid-twentieth century, pockets of composing work were clearly underway. For example, Ash and Rapaport (1957) advocate the composing of songs and tunes for children of junior age, giving examples of children's pieces. Again this approach is arrived at within the context of children's work in other arts. They also note that children who take a special interest in composing must be encouraged, and they outline the series of composing work done by one child over her last two years in junior school. However, even by the late 1960s, creative work in primary school music was in evidence only in the most patchy form. *The Plowden Report* on English primary schools noted:

> Exploration of sounds in their raw state is a useful first stage in independent creation, a first stage which many infant schools have reached, but the need for control, selection, discipline and technique soon arises if the work is not to become static and repetitive. It is easier to start improvisation than to continue it into the junior and secondary stages. Not enough is yet known about how to develop children's creative powers in music. Here, research is needed.
>
> (DES 1967: para. 692 d)

The report made explicit comparison with work in other subjects:

> In many schools mass instruction is given in music, and in music alone, to whole classes or even combined classes: little is attempted in groups or by individual method, and teacher direction persists in this field even in schools where it has almost disappeared in language, maths and art. . . .
>
> The planning of music as a creative subject lags behind work in language and the visual arts and crafts.
>
> (DES 1967: para. 692 a and d)

Some teachers, however, through making the same comparisons, had been transferring the approaches used in other areas to music with considerable success. In 1974, Glynne-Jones published a book, *Music*, which contains an extensive account of children's musical development, largely through discussion of the composition work of the children she was teaching at the time. She takes a Piagetian approach to the cognitive development evident in children's music through the early and middle years of schooling. This text is still among the very few focusing attention on the music children make themselves, presented in notation, and showing how teaching approaches can be based upon this. In her opening discussion, Glynne-Jones writes:

> In recent years there has been a liberation in children's painting and writing activity, with remarkable work produced by ordinary, not especially gifted children. We now know that if their environment stimulates and feeds children's imaginations, they become writers and painters within their own society. . . . The beginnings of musical expression are present for all to see in the activity of young children, but somehow it is put off-course and seldom develops in the same way as other forms of expression. This must inevitably be attributed to the experiences of children in school.
>
> (Glynne-Jones 1974: 9)

Glynne-Jones' argument is that music teaching must be based, like any other teaching, on an understanding of children's wider development. It is indicative of the state of music teaching that a case should have to be made for this and that, to this day, this principle is little in evidence in music curriculum planning. The children's own music is observed through many examples and discussion of their development is based on the insights gained. This book has as much to say to us, almost thirty years on, as it did when first published, particularly in the implicit model it gives of a teacher who listens to children's work.

What seems extraordinary in hindsight is that such work did not become more consistently widespread across primary schools. A clear factor in this is the issue of who was doing the music teaching. Where music remains separate from the rest of the curriculum in the hands of music specialists, it is often the composing aspect that suffers most, or is left out altogether. While primary class teachers have a close knowledge of their children and experience of teaching in other creative areas, the music specialists may be at a disadvantage on both counts. More significantly, however, they have their own musical training to deal with.

From the teacher's point of view, the development of composing as part of the mainstream music curriculum has not been without its problems. One of the most uncomfortable of these has been the realisation on the part of many music teachers that their own specialist training was based almost exclusively on the performance or study of already-existing music, so that the idea of composing one's own music appears somewhat alien, not to say daunting. And, strangely one might think, even the study of already-existing music has often offered little insight into the processes of its making, concentrating instead on the finished 'object', whether sung, played, analysed or written about. All this has two opposing consequences: a tendency to see composing as of rather low status and value, particularly in comparison with performing, and a paradoxical tendency to see composing as reserved for a very small and talented elite and therefore simply untouchable. Here again all the issues of how composing is viewed by the community at large come into play. The resulting lack of knowledge, experience and confidence in music specialists has made the teaching of composing hard for many to come to terms with. This may go some way towards explaining why some of the most positive teaching of composing has been done by primary class teachers, many of whom would claim not to be 'musicians'. Their success has been achieved by drawing on their knowledge of children's general development and on teaching skills transferred from approaches already familiar in eliciting art, creative writing or dance from children.

During the 1970s, composing at last began to find its way into the mainstream secondary curriculum. Gradually the teaching focus moved more towards the music pupils were producing themselves, its value and qualities, and its sound. In England, the Schools Council Project, 'Music in the Secondary School Curriculum', directed by John Paynter and based at the University of York, published its first Working Paper in 1974. The paper, by Piers Spencer, was entitled *The Influence of Pop on Creative Music in the Classroom*. It was based on discussion of a set of examples of compositions by 14 and 15 year old pupils, and included recordings of their music. The Schools Council Project, through the decade or so of its existence and later dissemination stages, contributed enormously to teachers' understanding of secondary pupils' capabilities in composition. Although its brief was to look at secondary school music as a whole (Paynter 1982), and the range of practice it gathered together and generated through working papers and conferences covered all aspects of the music curriculum, developments in composition come through as a strong element in much of the work. The project was undoubtedly a major influence in composition becoming a compulsory area of the music curriculum when the national criteria for the new examinations in music at 16-plus were published in 1985 (Paynter 1981). Throughout the project, access was made available to examples of teachers working with composition in a variety of settings. Most importantly, these examples included aural and video recordings of the music of pupils from age 11 up. Here at last was a major gathering together and consideration of the musical work of pupils in school, in which there was considerable emphasis on the music that students themselves composed, recorded and performed.

Through the Project's endeavours, the sound of children's work in composition became much more widely heard among teachers and extensive debate and curriculum development based on this followed. Teachers were arguing cogently for the place of composing in the curriculum and were taking children's composing seriously at a much deeper level than before. Gamble writes as a secondary music teacher:

> Children's compositions function simultaneously as both ends and means: they have intrinsic value as unique, original, imaginative compositions

which should have aesthetic value for their peers, their teacher, their parents, or anyone else who cares to listen. At the same time these compositions help children to develop musical imagination and deeper understanding of their own expressive objects as well as the work of other composers.

(Gamble 1984: 16)

Gamble's work at Manland School, Harpenden, made composition the central activity of the music curriculum, but contextualised it within a detailed, rich and challenging series of investigations of musical techniques and devices. These were exemplified by encounters with music of many different kinds, including an array of contemporary and earlier twentieth century composers (Paynter 1982). Other teachers wrote in depth about the compositions of their pupils, in itself an indication of a considerable change in values. Loane (1984) approaches analysis of children's music from a theoretical perspective based on the work, among others, of Suzanne Langer, listening to their music as 'thinking in sound' and considering the musical structures in terms of their symbolic and expressive import. Bunting (1987, 1988) examines questions concerning the teaching of composition through detailed case studies of pupils' work over two and three term time-spans. The study of a series of pupils' work in this way opens up the ways in which their compositional working practices, skills and understanding develop through interactions with a teacher. This brought a new level of seriousness to the treatment of children's composing, becoming a widespread force in the main school curriculum.

As composing became a staple part of the curriculum for pupils in some quarters, its place in the examination system came under review. Composition – often in a rather curious relationship to pastiche writing in the styles of classical composers – had been an optional part of Advanced Level examination syllabuses well before it appeared in examinations at 16 plus. For some time, teachers who wanted to enter pupils at 16 plus for a music examination containing composition had to use the Certificate of Secondary Education (CSE), intended for pupils of lower ability than the General Certificate of Education (GCE), because the latter regional boards did not offer it at all. Under CSE, teachers could propose their own syllabuses for music and many used this framework to strengthen the composition element in the curriculum for pupils of this age (Bunting 1975).

With the introduction of GCSE (General Certificate of Secondary Education), composition became acceptable in England across the whole 16 plus system, and the music which pupils were composing was brought further to the fore in the quite ferocious debates which arose concerning the assessment of pupils' work. This did at least focus attention onto the music produced and, by extension, sometimes drew into discussion aspects of the processes by which the finished pieces had been arrived at. Inevitably in this context however, the emphasis was on the vexing question of how *good* the work was and what mark it should be given. This rather obscured wider, more fundamental questions of what the music was *like* at all, and where it belonged in relation to pupils' development. In those days too, most pupils started work on their examination syllabuses as more or less beginner composers, making it hard to tell what was characteristic of the age group and general musical experience, and what were simply features of the work of inexperienced composers. Teachers found that the problem of how to tell better compositions from worse was exacerbated by a number of factors. Differences in performance skills and theoretical musical knowledge had a considerable impact on some aspects of composing, since the principal working method was for pupils to make up the music by singing or playing it on the spot and then writing it down. Choice of style was problematic (Green 1990) as assessors struggled to compare fully fledged rock and pop songs with the kind of 'Melody for 'Cello' pieces based on music learnt from instrumental tutor books, or four-part harmony exercises with the stylistic rules relating to J. S. Bach's chorales temporarily suspended so that the work could be seen as composing rather than pastiche. A keen debate arose over whether assessment of music is possible at all. This drew on earlier debates concerning assessment in the arts (Smith and Best 1980).

All this was generating debate about musical values, but it still did not seem fully to take account of the pupils themselves or of what might be expected of young composers at primary or earlier secondary stages of music education. Strangest of all, from the educational point of view, was the apparent willingness to consider assessment questions concerning 14 to16 year olds with almost no reference to the development of much younger children's composing pathways. In this respect music educators again lagged great distances behind educators in other disciplines. How could achievement at 16 plus be targeted without any picture of what might go before? Here another paradox arose. In England at least, it was the place gained by composition in GCSE that was the final impetus for the inclusion of composing as a statutory part of the music curriculum for pupils from age 5 onwards. Yet this 'top down' approach has been probably the most damaging factor in the development of composing in schools since the 1980s. It is extraordinary that the planning for composing in the statutory curriculum made little or no reference to anything but the vaguest sense of what might be expected of young children's music, or of children's working processes. The consequence is a vast underestimation of what can be expected and a commensurate underachievement.

There is now a growing number of studies of children composing which have begun to build up the developmental picture so necessary for teachers planning for composing. These bring children's own music and music-making into the foreground in the search for ways to develop the teaching of composition so that it builds on a deeper understanding of children's work. Davies (1986, 1992) investigates children's song composing from a developmental perspective, looking also at the teacher's role. Upitis (1992) makes an extensive study of young children's composed songs and instrumental music, based on their use of emergent music notations and linking it interestingly to a 'whole language' approach which makes parallels with literacy development. Barrett (1996, 1997) looks at children's compositional processes from the point of view of aesthetic decision making, also using their invented notations as a way of gaining insight into musical thinking. Others, such as DeLorenzo (1989), Kratus (1989, 1994) and Wiggins (1994), have also researched aspects of children's compositional processes, working alone or in groups. Folkestad *et al.* (1998) are among those extending consideration of these processes to children's compositional work using music technology. Swanwick and Tillman (1986) propose a developmental sequence based on children's spontaneous improvisations and later more compositionally based work. Burnard (1999a, 2000) explores the intricate and complex relationships between improvisation and composition in the work of early adolescent pupils and draws conclusions concerning the implications for teaching. This book cannot do justice to the work of these and others in the field. Nor can it attempt another major enterprise much in need of further work, that of bringing the findings of those working in more specific fields of cognitive musical development (Bamberger 1991; Serafine 1988; Deliege and Sloboda 1996) much more directly to bear on pedagogical approaches to composing in schools.

Researchers looking at the music made by the youngest children – spontaneous song-making, improvising with instruments, singing and dancing together – are listening to the music that children apparently generate as simply a part of their normal repertoire of play behaviours. With encouragement this propensity for music-making works its way through into pre-composition and early composing work, as an emergent ability much akin to the acquisition and development of language. All children begin on this path and there is good reason to think that all will continue if the environment and climate are conducive to sustaining it. As is discussed later (Chapter 4), this early development seems to have its own momentum, which demands teaching approaches based on listening and scaffolding (Young 1995), and matching input to the individual moment and need, as well as the provision of a rich and stimulating musical environment. All this contributes to establishing a base-line understanding from which to build a picture of unfolding compositional development.

Meanwhile, researchers who are comparing the music-making of children and adolescents with models of musical invention which belong to the socially and culturally specific musical worlds of adult music see things from a quite different perspective (Bunting 1977; Shehan Campbell and Teicher 1997). These two perspectives tend to remain distinct from one another. This raises one of the central questions of this book, namely the crucial question of how young children's music-making 'languages' mature and transform into adult ones. Clearly children's composition cannot effectively be considered in isolation. From the earliest age the normal development of children involves a gradual enculturation into the adult practices of the social and cultural contexts in which they are growing up. Innate musical inventiveness unfolds in interaction with the child's immediate cultural surroundings. Teachers can support compositional development by building musical awareness and understanding, by supplying skills and technique, and by extending children's experience of the contemporary musical world in which they live.

Children's music opens our ears to a whole dimension of aural experience too rich to be lost. All music makes audible something of the imagination, the physical being and the soul of the maker. All music arises from the lived experiences and perceptions of the human society to which it belongs. As a community we have no substitute for the music children create. Teachers can only begin by listening.

Chapter 3

Listening to children's music

Listening to children 'musicking', as Small (1998) might term it, is a strange business. Yet, as teachers working with children making their own music, this is literally all we have. The skills of listening are central to all music teaching. Being there, listening and following what happens, is the bit for which there is no short cut. As a time-based art, the musical experience is here and then gone. While we're hearing it, music is felt on the body and lived through in real time, immediately. Cage (1978) gets hold of the essence of musical experience at its best when he says:

> What it
> is is theatre and we are in it and
> like it, making it.
> *(42' 40" in 45' For a Speaker)*

Afterwards, we can only re-live the music in mind or listen again. The invisibility of music makes it hard to reflect on: aural images cannot easily be shared in discussion with the children. Although a notation or score of some kind can help map the music so that it can more easily be grasped, teachers and children are still faced with the demands of having to hear it 'in the head'. And this returns us to the activity of listening in the first place: listening, remembering, and trying to hold on to the experience in some lasting form. For the teacher, listening is the means of access; it is listening for the sake of the musical experience itself, but also listening in order to learn what the child is doing, to remember the detail of what is heard, and to respond with insight and empathy.

I have written elsewhere about the process of listening to children's music as giving a window onto their musical understanding, their music-making being essentially a form of 'thinking aloud' (Glover 1990; Glover and Ward 1993/8). During the earliest stages of a long study of children's composition, which started by tracking the self-devised composition work of 100 children, aged 7 to 11, through their school summer term, my perceptions of what this listening role entailed changed considerably. From a concentration at the outset on collecting on tape the 'products' of children's composition – songs and instrumental pieces – it became obvious that listening to these afterwards as if they were stand-alone 'musical objects' went only a small part of the way towards gaining insight into the music itself. It was as if the 'piece' was only the shell left behind after the real inner event was over. Listening 'live' and listening later are quite different experiences. The analytical approaches based on listening to disembodied music, which are predominant in so much formal musical training, are just not enough. This is because the context in which the music is made, the sources drawn on for ideas, and the children's wide range of purposes for their music are all so intrinsic to their work that, for teaching purposes at least, listening to the music needs to encompass some understanding of all this. The listening approach that is needed must be broad-based and as free from preconceptions as possible.

Different perspectives

If, as listeners, we want to gain some insight into children's music, we have to try to understand it from the perspective of the child as well as our own. This, of course, is no different from the way we might approach the music of any composer new to us, or music of a kind or a place or a time that we have not encountered before. And we can take as a starting point the fundamental relationship between all composers and their audiences, grounded as it is in the different perceptions of the music as offered and received. Listening to, and becoming familiar with, children's work can be seen as part of the same process of coming to understand that applies to all new musical encounters. Listeners bring their own musical experience and understanding to what they are hearing, influenced by their personal and cultural musical biography. This understanding may be stretched or challenged by the unfamiliar, which then demands an effort of accommodation and an attempt to shift perspective in order to enter more fully into the musical experience and to understand it better.

One of the unnerving aspects of this process when applied to very young children's music can be the need to strip away really fundamental listening habits in order to hear the music in its own terms. For example, a child may make a piece that is carefully and consistently structured rhythmically but played on almost random pitches because, for the child, the pitch is not the focus of attention. The adult listening may find it hard to hear through, as it were, their own habit of latching on to melody. This is not to suggest that the melodic aspects of the music can be ignored. Rather that, instead of hearing rhythm and pitch as inseparable, a clearer insight into the music will be gained by foregrounding the rhythm as structure, and hearing pitch with timbre as colour, and as shifting, changing colour at that. This is not so far from the difficulties earlier audiences had with the concept of *Klangfarbenmelodie* in the music of Schoenberg and Webern, though for different reasons. There may also be a need to widen the conception of listening altogether. Young suggests that a more multi-sensory approach is needed, particularly in relation to instrumental music.

If we listen to and study children's music-making on instruments with our aural sense alone as merely sonic productions then we are understanding it within the conventional definitions of music in an adult's world. To immerse ourselves in a child's world of sound is to become drawn into a process of listening operating through many sensory channels of communication simultaneously. We will allow a kinaesthetic response to be sympathetically felt in our own bodies, incorporate the visual information with the listening experience, respond to the music as part of the making and maintaining of connections between ourselves and the children.

(Young 1995: 54)

Adults listening to the music of children are differently placed from adults listening to adults' music, or children listening to each other. There is a disparity of perception due to maturity and musical enculturation which is there, whether or not the listener is musically trained, and it is a disparity which needs to be recognised when working with children. Interestingly, this applies as much to listening to the music of adolescents as it does to the very youngest age groups. With older students, it can be harder to realise this, particularly if their ability as performers outstrips their experience as composers and listeners.

The gulf between how the adult hears the music and the perceptions the child may have of what he or she is doing relates to developmental aural awareness. More fundamentally perhaps, this is also the near edge of the question of what a child is intending for, or intending in, the music. The question of intentions operates at each level, from the most detailed aspects of the musical construction to the most general. This gulf can be illustrated by R's music for tambour (see page 51) which poses issues typically raised by young children's music.

As the teacher, I listen to the stream of this child's repeating musical pattern. Transcribed onto a page it might be analysed as an anacrusis of two crotchet beats, followed by a straight 3/4 bar and then the remainder (two quavers and a crotchet) of the 4/4 bar which leads back to the anacrusis; an alternating pattern of threes and fours, clearly defined in the accenting. This is metrically interesting, given that most of what this 5 year old sings is grouped in straight fours, sometimes threes. 'Interesting', that is, in relation to an adult's musical understanding.

R said: 'I do: scrape scrape bang, scrape scrape bang-bang bang'.

(Glover 1998: 137)

Both descriptions of the music are accurate, yet they conflict almost entirely in terms of the aspects of musical understanding brought to bear on the 'musical thinking', and in terms of the different 'takes' of child and adult on what is going on. Essentially for the child, as best we can tell, this is an *action* piece (Glynne-Jones 1974), conceived of in terms of 'what I do'. For R, the musical focus at the time appeared to be the fascination of the contrast in timbre between the scrape action and the bang. The patterning is intrinsically kinaesthetic, with an accompanying aural enjoyment of the sound of sound, well recognised developmentally as of early importance to children musically (Moog 1976). The rhythm is felt as much as heard from within the body action, displaying the short-short long pattern, also well recognised as an early feature, and the metre arises in a most natural way from the numerical mix of actions and accenting. These rhythmic aspects seem to be enjoyed within the bones, as it were, intuitively.

The problem is trying to listen to this music from within the child's understanding of it, and this includes consideration not only of what happened but also of what was intended. This may be the musical intention at the level of musical patterning and structure, as above. It may also be something much more general in terms of the whole conception of the music, on this occasion something like 'I'm playing with the drum; I'm doing the music, now'. The first is a purpose *in* the music, the second a purpose *for* the music. Both might affect how we listen to and how we hear the music.

Listening to children composing

A key starting point in listening to children's music is, then, the ability to de-centre from one's own perspective and to try to hear the music in the terms in which it is offered. For the teacher who is to enable children's composing to progress and develop, four aspects come into play in relation to a listening approach.

1   The musical experience and creativity a child brings into the work; this is often accessible only through the music itself, either aurally or in the ways it is produced.
2   The purposes or intentions the child has in making the music; these can only be deduced or even guessed at with the help of observation or perhaps talk.
3   The music-making process itself, how it is approached and what is entailed; here direct listening and observation can contribute considerable insights, given time and access.
4   The music as made and heard: played, sung or technology-based, live or recorded.

Together these thread through discussion in the following chapters of this book, particularly as they take on different features as children develop and move into new age phases. Each is fundamental to an understanding of the many different kinds of composing children do. And for each, listening offers an important perspective.

Musical experience

A useful mainstay in approaching children's music as a listener is to begin always by listening for what *is* there, as opposed to what isn't. One of the things that can come through quite strongly in the music itself is the previous musical experience the child brings to it. This may be in the audible shape of technical skill in managing musical elements or structures such as rhythm and metre, melody shape or tonality. More often, and with even the youngest children, it is just an intuitive grasp of musical features, procedures or forms. The music itself shows what has already been grasped or selected from music that has been heard, played, sung or danced to. Since consciously or unconsciously children work towards making sense of music, and since their aural acuity is often extremely sharp and detailed, they assimilate a considerable amount from what they have heard around them. Listening to their music can tell us what they have met before.

When children arrive in school and are in the music classroom for the first time, the attitude sometimes taken is that the task of building their musical understanding starts here. It is easy to see how this happens. The teacher of 4 and 5 year olds may be faced with a large class whose vocal and instrumental skills are in early stages and who have a limited vocabulary with which to talk about music. Suddenly there seems little or nothing to go on, and it is not easy to uncover the understandings children bring from their diverse backgrounds and experiences. Unless some open-ended music-making opportunities are available, their wider understanding of what music is and what it can do is not called up. Neither is there room for them to show their intricate set of perceptual skills and intuitive understanding, the acquisition of which is well under way for most children by this age. The assumption may be made that for children to invent their own music at this stage is a tall order and that only the most detailed and structured tasks, firmly led by the teacher, will be possible. In fact, the music children of this age make by themselves, if the opportunity can be offered, is a powerful means of accessing the musical understanding which appears missing. An experienced listener can take full advantage of this and such listening does not need specialist musical training. Seen in the wider context of the ways in which early years teachers are used to accessing and then building on the understanding children bring in other fields – language or mathematics, for example – parallel strategies can be transferred into the sphere of music.

Each time children move to a new teacher, and particularly at the points of transfer between schools, the difficulty reappears. Understandably perhaps, as the range of differing musical experiences grows, teachers find it easier to assume that the 'beginning' is the safe place to start. Pupils are returned to tasks that demand, and therefore produce, little, creating a kind of self-fulfilling lack of expectation. The difficulty is that the real beginnings were already underway before the child could even speak. Once again, if open-ended composing activities are not made available alongside the kind of class work that allows pupils to work in different ways and at their own levels, a teacher will not uncover the full extent of each individual's abilities. If pupils are encouraged to set and work towards their own next level of challenge, teachers can gain access through listening to the ways in which students are understanding their music and what their capabilities are, both creatively and technically.

S (aged 8) selected a pair of small bongo drums and sat down cross-legged to play. His arm, hand and finger movements immediately showed that he was basing his music-making on the actions of a tabla player he saw each week at the temple. This of course had a direct bearing on the music produced, full of different levels of dynamic attack, flurries of ornamentation and periodic indications of the feeling of arrival that accompanies the beginning of each rhythmic cycle in the musical tradition to which this playing referred. Where S. situates himself as a 'composer' is modelled on music-making within his most immediate experience. In his head, he is drawing on a set of images completely different from those of R (page 23).

What it is to 'make up your own music' is clearly relative to the musical culture in question. Researchers and teachers cannot assume a single, standard definition of what composing is and expect that this will be common to the experience of all pupils. Clearly, children bring with them whatever they have absorbed from the mix of musical cultures to which they have been exposed: ethnic, religious, folk, art, popular and all sub-cultures between. Improvising with hand drums standing-in for tabla (seen earlier), making up a country and western song (like your dad), and composing a flute piece (like the ones you play in lessons) are purposes conceived from inside completely different cultural perspectives and give totally different sets of bases for compositional decision-making. Where children's pieces are clearly and directly related to cultural models, as S's music was, they are easy to recognise even if they pose the listener a problem of unfamiliarity. But this is not always the case. Because children are inexperienced, their musical equivalent of a first or home language is not neatly parcelled into appropriate genres and formats; it just *is* the musical stream they know. So there is a shifting relationship between how they draw on what they know in music-making and how this is accommodated to immediate purposes. There can also be major differences from one child to another in how close a composing task in school comes to anything culturally familiar. The teacher may be operating on a single, assumed, compositional model, as if it was culturally neutral but this is never the case. This too must affect how we hear children's music.

Musical purposes and intentions

It was with the aim of gaining insight into what children produce when working on entirely self-devised composing projects that I set up the study introduced earlier, in which one of my main objectives was to become a more astute listener to the music children make. This first study was carried out in a multi-ethnic city junior school. An empty classroom in the school was turned into a permanent composing base, stocked with a not very luxurious range of instruments. This operated on an open-access basis for most of the school day. I worked with each class on a more formal 'music lesson' each week, so that the children encountered me at those times in an ordinary teaching role. For the remainder of the work, I simply provided opportunity, equipment, a recording facility, and a listening ear when required. Children were free, within only the constraints of being released from class, to choose when to come to make their music, how often and for how long, and also to choose what music-making they engaged in. This was the nearest it was possible to get within a school situation to offering children the opportunity not only to use their own ideas within the music itself, but also to devise and pursue their own musical purposes or intentions. The children were relatively inexperienced as instrumentalists and within the school context 'making up your own music' was new to most of them. So the group, though spread across the age range, was constituted mainly, from a school point of view, of beginner composer/improvisers. All the children in the school were included and all took up the composing opportunity in some way.

The music was recorded on day-to-day tapes that were a mixture of work in progress, single event improvisations, and completed pieces, some in several versions as they were repeatedly re-visited over time. Some children chose to make their music much more often than others. An overall aim was to create a sense of ongoing opportunity which would allow music-making to be just one thing among others, rooted as much as possible into the ordinary round of daily life. The study was later extended in a number of ways, including weekly visits to work with younger children (aged 5–7) in the same neighbourhood, composition projects of varying lengths in other settings and work by other teachers with their own classes.

In 1984, it did not seem very radical to offer completely open opportunities for children to find their own compositional starting points. Although the framework I set up offered a facility that is hard to recreate on the same scale in an ordinary school situation, some such provision is, I believe, both practical and essential to composing development. More recently, there seems to be an increasing reluctance to allow pupils to compose outside the limits of a pre-set task. The rationales for this are sometimes pragmatic – time, space, equipment – and sometimes educational. It may be felt that without a given starting point children won't know what to do, or that without a given starting point teachers don't know what to do with what children do. More usefully, there are debates about the ways in which imposed constraints challenge pupils to think creatively or help them to discover new possibilities. I would subscribe to the latter points, but commissions need to be balanced by self-initiated composing, whatever the age group. For if children aren't encouraged to devise their own musical starting points, an essential aspect of their musical creativity is lost. Furthermore, it is when they come up with their own ideas for what the music will be that it becomes most meaningful to them. In my experience, this is often the point at which they really 'take off' as composers. What form the music will take is fundamentally determined only in relation to what a composer wants to explore or to do with it. To take away from pupils the expectation that they will have their own ideas about this is to turn composing into a kind of problem-solving activity from which the meaningfulness of the problem has been removed. It is like expecting pupils only to write what they are told to write, or using only the words or number of sentences they have been given.

One major advantage of the way I had set up this work (perhaps somewhat disreputably from a research point of view), was that the open access, and the availability of individual choice about when and what the music would be, gave the opportunity for much greater insight into where the children were 'coming from'. It had the effect of highlighting the range of 'purposes' they brought to their composing. As time went on, the chance for the children to revisit, to stay with an old idea or piece, or to go on to the next in the series also strengthened the aspect of devising purposes. Children began to think about their ideas for pieces of music in advance of coming to make the music; they had time to think about what might be possible, as well as to pick up ideas from each other or from our music lessons, and find new avenues to explore that way. They would come to tell me of an idea they'd had for the next piece they wanted to do. Or a child would say something like: 'I thought of some music when I was sitting on the bus. What I'm going to do is . . .' This is a strategic step forward in musical independence and in taking control and starting to think musically.

Based on music collected in this first study, the list below sets out some of the kinds of musical purpose children in this middle age-range seemed to adopt as a basis for their work at a general level. At the expressive or imaginative level, it is the music once made that has to speak for itself, and I hesitate to try to categorise these creative intentions into even broad compartments. Later chapters look in more detail at examples of children's work and more can be found on the website linked to this book. Only getting to know individual pieces as they are being made can really put the listener in touch with the music at the deepest level. The following list may help to show how children are in process of taking on board general musical categories that adults take for granted. As a listener, it is important to uncover these distinctions, however basic they seem, without prior assumptions as to what is going on.

Just playing/singing

Some of the music made is intended for no audience at all and is a direct engagement in singing and playing just for its own sake. As improvisation, this is a form of play (Hennessey 1998) and of making 'sound marks' on the environment. It may be accompanied by a commentary or, in the case of instrumental music, by singing along. Observable at all ages, it is not restricted to young children, although it is similar in character to much of what younger children do. The musical stream that results may be highly structured or more exploratory.

'I'm making some music'

By contrast, some of the younger children announce themselves as being quite consciously in charge of music as it's produced. The music may be anywhere on the spectrum between improvisation and composition, but there is a sense of making something that can be heard for itself, either by self or others. For older children, and adults, this would be taken as read.

Imitation

A clear intention in a number of cases is to imitate music-making a child has watched, as does S (page 26). This may be acknowledged or not. Composers are more or less as invisible as their music, so it is usually performers who become the model. The music is made through actions, energy and attitude that has been closely observed and borrowed. This directly affects how the music sounds. Sometimes the activity is characterised as pretending, as in 'I'm pretending to make a song'. Pretending is the intention, but the musical outcome is as real as any other.

Making a 'song'

There may be two meanings to this, one being that of making a song in the standard, vocal sense, the other that of making an instrumental piece, called a 'song' in a usage also found on drum machines and some composing software. In either case there is a clear sense of aiming for an overall structure and of music as 'object', something which can be constructed and then recognised as existing in its own right, and heard or performed by others as such.

Making patterns and structures

Here the actual construction is intentionally expressed, although generally in quite abstract terms. This is composing music that is based on doing something orderly with musical or other structures, such as number, action or visual structures. For example: 'I do two of this (note or chord) and three of that'. 'We put these (glockenspiels) opposite ways round then play the same' (inversions). 'I go all the way round and then bang in the middle' (T, page 51). The idea of the music is to put a conceptual plan into action, changing it if necessary. The plan may be pre-conceived or it may emerge from an improvisatory beginning.

Discovery of a musical idea

Often it is a musical idea itself that interests children enough to want to turn it into a piece. A melodic fragment, moving in parallel thirds or fifths with two beaters, or a broken chord pattern would be examples of this, focused on because they are discovered and enjoyed or found intriguing. The intention of the music then becomes that of making the idea into a whole piece.

Interaction

Sometimes the intention is to set up the music interactively: 'we're making music together'. This can extend to trying out models of linguistic interaction: 'this is a conversation', 'we're having an argument'; or into finding different ways to join forces. Musical structures are often essentially based on interaction of singers or players, taking turns or joining in.

Drama of sound

Dramatic or expressive intentions drive the musical construction. 'I'm making crying music' leads to a melody worked round very small melodic intervals; 'We are the Three Beaters' announces a piece of layered, vigorous drumming patterns.

Making music for a specific function

Music for dance, for sleep, for marching. For children, the function is often very particular to immediate circumstances, people or events.

Story, programme music

Songs that tell stories appear quite commonly in children's work, following the narrative structures of story-telling and ballads. Not a single example of instrumental music with a programme appeared until the penultimate week of the study. This seems to be an adult-led phenomenon, rather than something children come to for themselves. Its overemphasis by teachers can be very stunting to composing development.

Given that the children had no experience of making their own music in school, these ideas of musical purposes seem to be examples of those which are most straightforwardly acquired through enculturation, or that simply come from engagement with musical materials. These are the musical 'games' with which children are familiar and they represent quite a range of ways of going about the evolving of sounds into structures. The plurality of these strategies is crucially important. In this sense too, it cannot be assumed that 'composing' is one thing. It may seem like stretching a point to include some of the above categories under the heading of purposes. With older composers, these approaches might justifiably be seen as straightforward differences in working methods. But for younger or inexperienced children these can often be assumptions about what it is to compose, which therefore find their way into the fundamental purpose of musicmaking as the child construes it. The music produced is so much a function of these mindsets that they have to be reckoned with as important contextual factors in listening to it. And the differences in first-person standpoint of the child towards the music are strategic to understanding the musical outcome, to hearing the music for what it is.

There are clearly developmental factors in the extent to which the child is able to be purposeful about a given aspect of the music. Arguably more influential, however, are the experiences children have to draw on in conceiving their compositional purposes. This is highlighted, for example, in the comparison between the instrumental music of young children (under 6, say) and their vocal compositions. I have suggested elsewhere (Glover and Ward 1993/8) that vocal and instrumental composition are very different developmental pathways. It has been noted by other researchers (Davies 1992; Barrett 1998; Swanwick and Tillman 1986) that there is evidence from children's song composition that they can structure musical form earlier than generally supposed. In the case of song compositions, two components may be relevant here. The words in a song are arguably the holding form; children have a familiarity with rhyme and story structures as language usages known from the youngest age, and may be able to structure words sooner than they can structure music.

Beyond developmental factors, however, there is another dimension in learning to make music purposefully. To continue the example, children know how songs go, in every sense. They know what a song is, what you do with it, and what you can expect it to have in terms of structure. And they know many examples of songs that have certain recurrent musical behaviours: verses, verse and chorus, for example. They know this because they have been song 'users' from the youngest age. They have encountered songs as part of ordinary life in the contexts which give them meaning as a form of music. Compared with all this, what models do children have of what a xylophone piece is? Or a tambour piece? For the youngest children making instrumental music, 'I'm making this music' is an intentional activity which is understood as the outcome per se, with no sense of constructing a piece which stands as an 'object' in its own right, apart from the doing. So there may be an asymmetry of purpose between 'I'm making a song' and 'I'm making some (instrumental) music'. It looks as though a crucial factor in children's work is having models of usage on which to base their own compositional purposes. Listening to children's work can help give the teacher cues for the ways in which introducing new models can extend the scope of their music.

Music-making processes

Much insight into children's work can be gained by listening to and observing music-making in progress and both hearing and seeing how ideas evolve. To return to an earlier image, this is listening to children thinking aloud. For some of the youngest children, the stream of music made as sung or made as played is, indeed, all there is. The music they make is transient and, although it may be quite clearly structured, is often improvisational and evolved in the moment. Close listening, following the surface of the music and tracking the thinking as it unfolds, will often indicate how the patternings of the music arise, how ideas are repeated, transformed or left behind, and how the impact of the music itself feeds back into the making process as the child hears the musical drama unfolding. Listening without intervening can be an invaluable learning experience for the teacher.

The development of the skills associated with the processes of evolving music is central in learning to compose more effectively. A major part of any teaching of composing is helping pupils to become aware of the processes they use, to develop the skills they can use in these and to extend or adapt their composing strategies in order to realise their ideas more successfully. The range of working processes composers use is as broad as the range of musical styles and outcomes and it is unwise to attempt to teach any single model. Here again is an aspect of working with pupils where keying in to the way they work enables teaching to pick up on what is already happening and reinforce, extend or, if necessary, challenge it. The higher the awareness the pupils themselves have about the working processes they use in generating their own music, the more able they are likely to be to progress with their work. There are exceptions to this. As with any creative work, the relationship between intuitive knowledge and explicit analytical understanding is a delicate balance and bringing processes into awareness can be a setback. For most, it is a worthwhile stage in moving forward; for some it may be counterproductive. Either way, the best way for the teacher to keep in touch with what is going on is to track the making processes as an important part of listening to children's work.

In music, as a time-based art, of course, the making processes operate with a double edge. The activity of doodling with a musical idea, trying it in lots of different forms, is a process of experimentation in the making stages of a piece. But it can also be taken as a musical process of development or transformation which may well come to be the musical piece itself. For this reason, pupils and teachers listening together and discussing processes in the early stages of working on a piece can contribute greatly to the understanding of how music works in time. Different working processes can lead into investigations of very different kinds of musical construction. Processes of repetition, phasing and layering may lend themselves to minimalist kinds of construction such as might be heard in the music of Glass or Monk. Pupils can investigate these further by trying out the performing skills demanded or by developing recording and multi-tracking skills using music technology. Other processes for investigation might include: developing a single idea in order to build a section or a whole piece out of it; building on a bass riff upwards, or from a chord progression outwards; or trying out different mixes and blends of timbre and texture, in which small adjustments to the chemistry create quite significant shifts of musical effect. Listening to pupils' working processes enables the teacher not only to relate more easily to what children make, but also to help pupils contextualise it by making links to other composers' work.

At the more general level, listening can help trace the overall stages that pupils' work moves through as it evolves. Kratus looks at the differences in compositional processes used by 7, 9 and 11 year olds composing a 'song' for electronic keyboard. Kratus divides students' working processes into four categories: exploration, development, repetition and remaining silent. Measurements of the time spent on each are considered in relation to the age of the pupils and their ability to replicate their piece accurately by playing it twice at the end of the time allowed. On the basis of this Kratus proposes:

> These findings suggest developmental differences in children's strategies for composing music, and they also suggest that, as children grow from age 7 to 11, development and repetition become more prevalent compositional processes. The 7 year old subjects 'composed' primarily by trying one musical idea after another (exploration). . . . In other words, the creative act of composition for the 7 year olds was very similar to the act of improvisation and they used compositional time to explore new ideas rather than modify ideas. The 9 and 11 year old subjects, on the other hand, used significantly more development and significantly less exploration, and 11 year olds used significantly more repetition than did 7 year olds. These results imply that 9 and 11 year olds use compositional processes that are similar to those used by the adult composers. . . . The difference between adult composers and children is that adult composers possess a higher degree of enabling skills. . . . which allow them to shape their musical materials in a more sophisticated manner.
>
> (Kratus 1989: 17)

The nature of the composing task used in Kratus' study is so restrictive that it is hard to extrapolate findings from it in relation to the composing children do in their own time and when working from their own starting points. Further, the idea that composing processes will be common across a group of children seems strange in itself, since working patterns and ways of approaching tasks of any kind must be both varied between pupils and also connected to the differences in outcome that one would expect from a range of genuinely creative work. Nevertheless, it is useful to listen to pupils working while bearing these process categories in mind, and also to consider how the use of processes alters with age and experience.

As attention turns to tracking and investigating the process aspects of children's composing, an interesting light is shed on these by using computer technology to store pupils' working interactions for later examination. One such study (Hickey 1997) suggests that middle-years subjects in the 'high creativity' group of those working on a computer-composing task 'showed a variety of musical manipulation skills (such as variation and sequence) and the ability to come up with new and musically interesting ideas quickly'. Naturally, the values applied are relative to the measures of creativity used, but such study alerts us to the need to consider what it is that helps pupils become more skilful as composers. Other researchers have looked at children's compositional processes from the perspective of problem-solving behaviour. DeLorenzo examined 11 year old students' decision-making processes, identifying four characteristics that seemed to guide these:

> (a) perception of the problem structure – the openness with which students perceived the creating task, (b) search for musical form – the degree to which students allowed the musical events to determine the form of the music, (c) capacity to sense musical possibilities – the depth to which students developed and shaped musical events, and (d) degree of personal investment – the level of absorption and intensity with which students engaged in the creating process.
>
> (DeLorenzo 1989: 193)

The findings of this study suggest that the extent of students' exploration is related to their perceptions of the range of choice within a task. They adopt a number of different types of strategy as a basis for 'shaping musical thoughts into a communicable product', with an interesting comparison emerging between those who use a 'pre-existing structural form' such as a storyline and those who allow 'the musical material to determine the form of the composition'. The latter demonstrate 'increasing concern for the musical relevance of each sound gesture' whereas the former spend more time practising and less 'thinking about the musical substance of the piece'. Students differ in their abilities to 'think in sound' and therefore to exploit the opportunity to evaluate, develop or transform sounds into expressive musical ideas. Unsurprisingly, 'the more fully a student participated in the musical decision making process, the greater investment he or she demonstrated in the emerging creative product'. This study is useful in the way it examines compositional processes in a school music class setting. Again the categories themselves can be useful starting points for observation of and listening to children's music-making in progress.

A major issue in relation to working processes for children arises in connection with whether the music is made by an individual or in a group situation. Working in a group brings a whole set of process dimensions of its own. Nankivell, working as a composer who has a great deal of experience as visiting animateur in school-based projects, has researched the model of group composition, particularly in the context of primary classrooms. His approach traces group composing as a procedure which is used by musicians – amateur and professional – across a range of diverse musical styles and cultures. In the light of these models, he examines ways in which group composing is used in school. Nankivell suggests that it can be useful to see the process of composing as having two main components – *invention* and *arranging*:

> At the nuts and bolts level of composition (i.e. the actual practice of making up a new piece of music), it consists of

i) musical ideas which are
ii) arranged in a specific way

(Nankivell 1999a: 28)

In a booklet accompanying a Composer-in-Education project carried out in four schools in North Kirklees, Nankivell enlarges on this two-part idea of the composing process:

> All compositions have these two elements and I find it useful to divide them up in order to clarify different strengths within a group of composers. For instance, in many pop groups (from the Beatles to U2) the music is frequently created by an individual coming up with an idea (an invention – maybe the lyrics, a melody or a chord sequence) which is then fleshed out and developed by the rest of the group, along with their producer, usually someone with different and complementary skills.
>
> INVENTION   ARRANGEMENT
> *Individual*   *Group*
>
> (Nankivell 1999b: 3)

The demands made on the listening teacher by group work can be considerable. As well as taking in the overall effect of the music as a whole and the combined processes through which it is being evolved, the teacher has an interest in tracking the musical roles of the individuals in the group. Sometimes it is necessary to separate what is happening aurally in order to gain insight into each child's input and understanding. The challenge of this is perhaps greatest when individuals in the group are working alongside rather than with each other. They may just be pursuing their own ideas, or they may be too musically inexperienced to be able to make their own music in conjunction with anyone else. So a form of parallel composing emerges in which each makes their own piece but all do so at the same time. This puts the listener into a listening role that has no parallels within usual audience practices.

Finally, listening to musical processes can be done from inside the music, so to speak. A teacher can join in with pupils' improvisatory work, both listening and contributing. This gives another 'viewpoint', one which is explored more fully in the next chapter. There are parallels here with listening to children talk. A teacher may tune in to children's language by listening as an observer. Another dimension, and possibly deeper insights, can be gained through talking with the child, or, in this case, interacting musically.

Music as made and heard

Central to learning in composition at every level is the experience for composers of having the music they have made listened to by someone else.

Teachers can provide another 'ear', reflecting back the way in which they as listeners hear and make sense of children's music. Such feedback may confirm a composer's perceptions or come as a complete surprise. Either way, the teacher can help the child increase awareness of the music's structure, impact or potential, giving an aural 'viewpoint' against which the composer can make further judgements.

Teaching composing entails the attempt to work with young composers at the edges of their musical understanding, and, as has been argued earlier, this requires the same kind of de-centring as reading children's writing or looking at their art. The composer and the listener each bring their own musical understanding and experience to bear and it is on this ground that they meet, with the pupils' work audibly between. Comprehending children's musical understanding, or making the best effort we can to do so, is a key to the quality of any teaching interaction which is going to help a child move forward. It is the quality of listening, by both teacher and children, that will count most in the end if the work is to develop. Composing is learnt over time, through series of pieces in which the next and then the next idea is discovered, the next technique tried out, the next musical shape found which is expressively right for the composer's purpose in each different enterprise. The key to supporting this development is awareness in listening. On this is based the long process of bringing musical ideas into consciousness by naming, describing and discussing them as a continuing part of listening and making compositional decisions.

Much of what follows in the next few chapters is concerned with gaining an understanding of children's music as a listener in order to contribute more effectively to their compositional development. Before embarking on this, it may be useful to summarise some possibilities offered by the listening role any teacher has in relation to moving pupils' work forward. The ideas below are explored in more detail through the rest of this book.

The teacher can develop a listening-led approach to children's composing by drawing on the following strategies, adapting them as appropriate to the setting and age group:

- Providing open opportunities for pupils to make their own music, enabling the musical experience, knowledge and skills they bring from home and previous music learning to be uncovered and heard.
- Listening to children's music-making in progress: listening attentively and saying nothing, listening and responding with some feedback, listening and noticing features that can be built on through later input, listening by joining in.
- Listening to pupils' finished work: listening and remembering, listening and discussing or assessing with the pupil, listening and describing or giving feedback, listening later to a recording of the music, listening and notating or making some analysis, listening and noticing how the work relates to

earlier composing; listening and noticing features that can be built on or linked to the work of other musicians.

- Matching planned inputs based on listening to pupils' work so that ideas found in their music are noticed, responded to, conceptualised, or extended.
- Setting up further composing opportunities – individual, paired, small group or class, in school or as homework, linked to projects or instrumental lessons; mixing set tasks with self-devised composing and exploring composing processes and work in progress as well as outcomes; basing all this on shared listening.
- Organising practical procedures for presenting and saving finished work, making it available for later listening and review: saving work on tape, disc or mini-disc, or in notated form for performance; setting up listening forums for bringing and discussing work in progress; making recordings available for individual or class listening.
- Ensuring that individual pupils collect their work; developing pupils as a supportive audience group, bringing music to different audiences inside school and beyond.
- Assessing children's composing, involving pupils' self-assessment in relation to their learning and how the music works in its own terms.
- Listening to a wide range of live and recorded music with pupils in order to provide a stimulating musical environment.

Most important of all perhaps is the kind of holistic listening that we bring to any new musical experience. Being caught up in the expressive qualities, the drama of the moment, and the unfolding aural images can lift the classroom experience onto another plane. Here we can simply respond to the music and enjoy the journey on which we are taken.

Chapter 4

Music-making in the early years

'That isn't music!' (B, 5 years old). 'It is!' (M, also 5 and very indignant). M, with a pair of 'Indian' bells in his hand, is shaking them in a strong clear rhythm pattern. B, listening intently, hears randomly clattering bell sounds, bearing little relation to the fist action. After a few repeats of the rhythm pattern she interrupts, unable to contain herself, as if M must be made to understand that we can't be expected to listen if he's not going to give us music. There's not much room for adjudication here. Within their own perceptions, they're both right. M is making a pattern – it couldn't be clearer from where he is – inside the repetitive arm action that is governing the sound. It is a four square crotchet and quaver rhythm pattern, hard to mistake. He feels and hears it with the force of making it. He was also enjoying the vigorous jangling of the bells until interrupted. B hears sounds all over the place, the uncontrolled and uncontrollable bells; listening predominates over what she sees. Within her view of the edges of music, this noise falls well outside.

The incident has several features characteristic of young children's music-making: the musical stream, made as played; the organisation of musical sound by the patterning of body action; the gap between intention and realisation in sound; the difference between perception through doing and perception through listening. It highlights too the challenge for the teacher in working with children in the early stages of making their own music. Does even the intended patterning here 'count' as music, let alone the actual sound? What can be expected? Can young children compose? What does it sound like if they do?

Ages 4–7

This chapter and the next look at children making their own music across the age range from about 4 to 7 years. Whether or not teachers want to describe this music-making as composing is perhaps academic, but supporting children's music-making development through this phase is crucially important in laying the foundations for later composing. The age boundaries of 4 and 7 years are approximate ones, chosen here partly to match provision within the settings – nursery and infant classrooms – in which school-based music education takes place for this age-group. More importantly though, there is a developmental watershed for children compositionally, as in many other spheres, around the age of 7. This is the stage at which, from the child's perspective, the idea of a piece of music as something separate from the experience and process of making it is becoming established. From here on, children are increasingly able to produce music with an identity of its own as a repeatable, time-based structure, which can be saved, listened to, sung or played by others. Adults take the concept of 'a piece of music' for granted. It is a concept inherent in the idea of composition and particularly at the forefront of musical thinking in western and European folk, classical and popular musical traditions (Goehr 1992). For young children, including most within this age range, the concept of a musical 'piece' is relatively insecure. This is particularly so in relation to the music they invent, as opposed to music they listen to or learn to sing. M's music (page 38) isn't thought of as a 'piece', it is just 'music', made and then gone. At this stage too, the relationships between what is improvised or composed, free or patterned, invented or borrowed, are very fluid.

It is probably most useful, therefore, to see this phase as one of 'emergent' music, of pre-compositional development during which, if a rich, supportive musical environment is provided, a great deal of musical groundwork is done. As with much early years work, however, it is all too easy to underestimate the capabilities of young children. It is a mistake to dismiss the music young children make up as incoherent 'scribble', formless or chaotic. Nearly always, once attention is taken up with singing or playing, the musical stream that emerges is full of patterning and structure, rich and imaginative, and as much connected to the musical culture in which the child is immersed as is the language they use. And, in parallel with language, for most children in normal environments, by the age of 4 musical development is well on the way. The teacher has only to 'tune in' to discover this. Young children may not compose pieces but they undoubtedly make music; and it is music to be valued for its own qualities.

This chapter explores the music young children make for themselves, in play or free choice settings, and how teachers can respond to this. The music is vocal or instrumental or both combined, the two strands taking rather different developmental pathways. And there are some distinctions to be made between the music children make alone and the music they make together in groups. Chapter 5 looks at the emergence of children's earliest composing work and classroom provision for it. Central to all this is the belief that children's composing must be seen as a matter of each individual child's musical development, as is their art, writing, dance and any other creative work. While there are some general features which can be observed in the music-making of large numbers of children, the creative musical energy that drives the work is always in some way particular to each child working in their own way. S plays on the xylophone with the lightest of touches and an expression of wonder at each sound produced. M, always business-like, makes music which is straightforward and decisive. Taking the long view of compositional development, sustaining the characteristic musical energy of each individual is an important endeavour for teachers.

Observing and matching

As we have seen in Chapter 2, the starting point in any teaching of composition is to listen. This is nowhere more true than in working with very young children. Any preconceptions that children cannot make music until taught to do so can be shed at the outset. No teaching strategies, formal or informal, can succeed unless they are based on an understanding of how children generate their own musical ideas, an understanding that is built only through ongoing listening to the qualities and features of the music produced. Without a sense of the children's own independent relationship to music – their perceptions, constructions, feeling for and interests in it – it is hard for the teacher to provide the kinds of opportunities, encouragement and intervention that will sustain development and lead to honest progression. The degree of 'match' between the opportunities offered by teachers and what is observed of children's capabilities and, more subtly, of the nature of their music, is of key importance.

Such knowledge of children's music is only gathered by experience, observation and listening to the music being made 'live' and in action, as it were. This is the best of starting points with every new class. Like language, music offers the additional chance to interact with children and gain understanding from an inside perspective. And as with language, the opportunities for observing children's music are entirely bound up with ongoing activity day by day. We can only make sense of the musical practice of children by living alongside the music in its 'home' settings, until it is understood in the context of how it is lived, woven into all the rest. To begin with this can be rather like travelling as a stranger in a new and different culture.

It is all too easy for the early years teacher in school to overlook the fact that both vocal and instrumental musical invention are based on spontaneous play behaviours which the children have been practising for themselves, unguided, since birth. At best, supporting children's development is a matter of sustaining, as well as progressing from, these self-taught musical beginnings. The adult composer embarking on the creation of a piece of instrumental or vocal music crosses a distinct boundary between ordinary and specifically musical behaviours. For young children, this is simply more of a very familiar world of controlling and patterning sound with intense interest: a world in which language, music, play, movement and dance all merge. Murray Schafer, the Canadian composer and teacher, observes:

> For the child of five, art is life and life is art. Experience for him is a kaleidoscopic and synaesthetic fluid. Look at children playing and try to delimit their activities by the categories of the known art forms. Impossible. Yet as

soon as those children enter school, art becomes art and life becomes life. They will then discover that 'music' is something that happens in a little bag on Thursday morning while on Friday afternoon there is another little bag called 'painting'. I suggest this shattering of the total sensorium is the most traumatic experience of a young child's life.

(Schafer 1975: 15)

This echoes the findings of Moorhead and Pond, thirty years earlier, from the Pillsbury Foundation Studies (discussed later):

In the free, fluid and dynamic environment which the child's life demands there is no sharp line of division anywhere between musical and non-musical experience. For it is impossible to conceive of music in the child's world as separate from that world. The child does not conceive it so.

(Moorhead and Pond 1942: 39)

If the teacher can create an environment in which music is an integrated part of each day's activities, and in which children can continue to pursue music embedded in everything else, the quality of children's music can be maintained.

Opportunities and experience

As a broad overview, the foremost aims for work with children's own music during the 4–7 age phase might be:

- to sustain children's spontaneous music-making abilities and encourage them to build on these with growing awareness
- to increase the musical skills, understanding and vocabulary which will support development in improvising and composing
- to do both the above in a musical environment which will enrich, interest and challenge children in pursuing their own creative work.

Achieving these depends on keeping a balance between plenty of quality opportunities for children to make their own music, and a rich provision of other musical experiences planned so as to extend their ideas, imagination and capabilities. These are brought together through listening and talking about music-making, the children's own and other people's. In this way, awareness grows and children come to see their work as developing and moving forward.

If children are to be able to continue the musical 'work' which is already underway when they arrive in a nursery or reception classroom, the opportunity for free play is essential. Organisationally, provision for free play in an open setting usually belongs more to a nursery or kindergarten setting than to classrooms for older children. This chapter is concerned with those situations in which children play freely in a planned environment that offers a variety of equipment, some of which may be specifically for music. Teachers or assistants take a flexible role, at times able to observe, listen or to take an interactive part in children's music-making. This partnering role is invaluable in relation to music play. Although opportunities for teachers to take such a role become less frequent with older groups, it is a musically sound method for teachers of any age group. The interface between play with music and musical improvisation is an intriguing one and the way interactive structures become musical ideas, relationships and transformations is a huge and important part of the way any music is experienced and understood.

Observing musical play

Music-making can be heard as part of children's play activity of almost any kind to a degree that often surprises even experienced observers the first time they look specifically for it. In the playground or the classroom, almost any play will be found to have musical aspects to it that easily become musical moments in themselves. Broadly, musical play behaviours fall into two categories.

- voice play, which might accompany almost any activity, still or moving
- 'instrumental' play in which objects or instruments are used musically, as an end in itself or accompanying other activity or movement.

The distinction between music made with the voice and music made with other instruments is a crucial one in relation to young children's music. Vocal and instrumental music arise in quite different ways and seem to have different wellsprings.

Musical play with the voice is intrinsically tied-up with language use and development as well as reaching beyond this to all kinds of vocalisations. Young children range freely along the spectrum of voice use, moving between:

- free vocalisation
- nonsense play with language
- speech
- chant
- sing-song
- song.

As children mature, these different uses of the voice become distinct and the free use of voice is lost. In early childhood almost any activity may incorporate language use that is essentially musical, and which moves between chanting, singing and song-making. This may take the form of original invention or it may draw on known songs or song fragments. Any movement activity, small or large, also brings with it singing and other vocalisations, or the playing of a portable instrument, actual or improvised. The deep-rooted connection between moving and 'sounding' is of prime importance as a source of young children's musical expression. These parallel modes of time-based activity seem to be intrinsically connected.

Z and F, twins aged just six, are playing 'Pirates' in the bath. The whole
episode continues for nearly half an hour, during most of which there's a
running commentary as the drama develops with boats and gold, pirates,
kings, queens and an octopus, and a good deal of splashing. This is high
drama, death and glory, with a wedding and some very narrow escapes from
drowning.

The narrative unfolds through every shade of voice use from speech to song,
both solo and in dialogue. Something of this range can be seen in the extract
below (page 44). 'We've got it' starts off as a chant on word rhythms using the
whole tone and minor third melodic shapes so characteristic of 'universal' chant
patterns. This turns into a ceremonial song style as the 'little mini man' is
announced king. Dialogue follows, interspersed with humming fragments which
follow actions (see below) and then turn into a wordless 'dance' number with a
strong clear rhythm: 'di di di di'. After more spoken explanation and some
humming, 'Hooray' is a full song in clear key and 4/4 time, which owes much of
its shape to the song 'Oh where and oh where has my little dog gone'. Yet it is
sung in a style completely befitting major national ceremonial events. Even
more triumphant is the final salute to the king and queen, using repetition to
build up the feeling of grandeur.

Music fitting the purpose is all of a piece with the story telling and enact-
ment. As with any music theatre form – opera, musical, dramatised story telling
– different musical levels and styles colour and heighten the drama. In this
quite spontaneous music, we can hear the twins launching into music that intuitively draws on the language use, drama and movement that generates the
musical motifs. At the same time they show how much experience they have
already gained through enculturation: of song structures, conventions of song,
dance and word rhythms, and musical fitness for purpose as absorbed within the
prevailing culture.

On the purely instrumental side, a similarly wide variety of activities may
involve spontaneous play with sounds made by striking, shaking, blowing or scraping objects of any kind in ways that lead into musical patternings. Once found
these patternings take over and are continued for their own sake. From the point
where the infant becomes interested in controlling the random sounds a rattle
makes when shaken, for instance, the use of objects as instruments – that is, as
extensions of body action to produce purposeful sounds – develops with a kind of
intrinsic motivation. Within the school context this behaviour rapidly fades away
unless some allowance is made for it. It is often discouraged as a general behaviour,
for obvious reasons, and if restricted only to those occasions on which instrumental performing is formally organised, it easily becomes pedestrian and stilted.

As an observer of musical play, the first thing to get accustomed to is picking
up and following what is essentially a stream of music, rather than a clear-cut
piece or event. Often the child moves between different kinds of musical
'episodes' and between music and not-music, all on the wing. A listener waiting

[Z and F, just six, play in the bath with boats and figures.]

Z: Where's my boat gone?

F:

We've got it, we've got them all from the pi-rate; a lit-tle mi-ni man saves us all from the lit-tle mi-ni boat; the lit-tle mi-ni man is now our king.

F: Zoe, he says he's got the gold and the boat from the water so he's going to be crownded king.

F&Z: (humming) Mm mm mm mm mm mm mm mm mm mm mm mm mm.

F: He's being gaven a great long train.

Z: Mine's decided to go upside down again, he's going under:

(staccato and dance-like, pitches approximate)
Di di di di di di di di di di di di di di di di di di.

Z: He did rather a silly thing; he got the right way round again. Now he's pressed the button to go the right way round again. He's toppled right off the boat... into the sea. Then:

(humming)

F:
Hoo-ray the pi-rate is so gone for our hon-our of the queen. He saved the land, he saved the land of our own it makes...

Z: The pirate's got in the boat again. He's safe and sound. Got into a little bed on his boat...

F:
Our king, our queen, the queen, yes the queen is now a queen of the land of Woe.

F: But it's falling!

z: Ow!

Figure 4.1 Pirates in the bath

for a clear-cut beginning and end may have a long wait. Secondly, making sense of the music will often demand taking into account the whole situation. Without the context that gives rise to particular patternings or expressive features, it is not so easy to latch on to the musical structuring itself. This is because, as adult listeners, our priorities are different from the child's in terms of how we hear the music itself.

> N (aged 4), or rather N's bear, is moving bricks from a pile at the side of the carpet into a truck. The bear picks up each brick and swoops it through the air before loading it into position. Each phrase length in the accompanying wordless song is linked to the varying length and pathway of 'swoop' in fetching the next piece of brick. This gives a pattern of different length phrases, accounted for initially just by the actions.

In a case like this, the music is simply invented on the wing to go along with a repetitive action. As the activity continues, the child is often exploring both music and action together. Here, what sets out as a focus on moving bricks to a truck becomes a holding structure for trying out the feel and the sound of shorter and longer routes. In effect, each 'route' is a musical phrase, shaped in length, pitch and dynamic. This belongs to a very important kind of musical work in establishing cause and effect. Getting to know that 'doing this, sounds like that' is a major part of children's exploratory musical activity.

It may also help the listener to realise that there is a very fluid relationship for the child between music that is being made up and music already known. Fragments of music previously heard or sung are often borrowed into the making process; rhythms, words or melodic ideas may be copied, extended or transformed as part of the musical stream of invention. This is particularly noticeable in song making where recognisable bits of other songs appear in 'pot-pourri' fashion from as early as 2 or 3 years old (Moog 1976; Hargreaves 1986). This can be seen in the 'Pirates' episode described earlier.

Children's music in play settings

There is surprisingly little research into the detail of children's musical play in ordinary settings. Even today, one of the most substantial studies of young children's musical behaviours in a largely free setting is the one carried out under the auspices of the Pillsbury Foundation in Santa Barbara, California, from 1937 to 1948. This is an extraordinary piece of research, particularly since it took place over some years in a school entirely set up for the purpose. Interestingly, the suggestion to do this came from the conductor Leopold Stokowski. The aim was 'to study the music of young children to discover their natural forms of musical expression and to determine the means of developing their musical capacities, particularly in the field of spontaneous creation'

(Moorhead and Pond 1941). The children, aged between 1½ and 8½ years old largely had the freedom to choose their own activities within a well-equipped general nursery school environment. Alongside play equipment, woodworking and gardening tools, a sandbox, and a garden and playhouse, provision included an extensive collection of musical instruments from all over the world. A phonograph and records were also provided, and the music for listening and dancing to including 'recordings of music from plainsong to Hindemith and the folk music of . . . twenty eight different countries – European, American, African and Asiatic' (ibid.). The Director of the nursery school was Gladys Moorhead, a Los Angeles primary teacher and child development expert. The Music Director was Donald Pond, an English composer who had worked at Dartington Hall School and in New York in the Children's Theatre Arts workshop and Dalton schools (Wilson 1981).

Moorhead and Pond published three substantial papers on the music of young children (1941,1942 and 1944) which together with a final article on the *Free Use of Instruments for Musical Growth* (Moorhead, Sandvik and Wight 1951) outline the observations made during the school's existence. These papers contain numerous examples of children's music in transcription and make a contribution to research in this field that is unparalleled half a century later. The focus of the work on children's own musical production is itself remarkable, as is the willingness to give time and non-interventionist attention to the observation of children's spontaneous musical creativity. It is perhaps not insignificant that this was the collaborative work of an educator and a composer.

In analysing and categorising the music collected at the school, Moorhead and Pond make two sets of basic distinctions. The first is that between vocal and instrumental music. The second concerns music produced 'in solitude' and music which arises from a group of children playing together. This distinction is noted in both vocal and instrumental music and it is based not just on numbers participating, but on a contrast in features of the musical style.

> One variety of instrumental music was flexible and asymmetrically measured rhythmically; it endeavoured to explore wide intervals in pitch and contrasting tone colours. Another was rigidly and symmetrically 'rhythmic'; it seemed indifferent almost to melody or to colour variation; it was insistent and savage. One was most frequently quiet and produced in solitude, the other raucous, associated very often with physical activity and belonging to the group. So also with vocal music. One variety was unfettered and free rhythmically like plainsong; the voice wandered over a large compass, the singer sang to himself alone, quietly, of everyday things, as though the melody not the words were more important. Another variety was rhythmic, like a ritual chant; the voice clung to one note around which it wove a melodic pattern limited in scope and insistent in form; it was sung most often in the group, usually loudly, repeated over and over again, rising often to a high emotional pitch.
>
> (Moorhead and Pond 1941: 8)

This description has a clear underlying flavour of seeing young children's group music-making as somewhat 'tribal'. Indeed, the implication that every developing child to some extent draws on some fundamental and primary musical 'voice', universal to humankind, runs through the Pillsbury commentaries. The phenomenon of even the youngest of children coming together as a musical unit, seemingly out of the blue, is well recognised. A teacher in a nursery describes four 2 year old boys playing randomly with an assortment of chime bars: 'But when one boy was at each bar, they took away the music, playing altogether, came to a stop, looked one another in the eye, raised both fists in air and said "Yeah!" Then they did it again.' The passage from Moorhead and Pond also brings out how different musical elements – timbre, rhythm, melody – take a more or less prominent part in different kinds of music, a point that holds true in my experience.

Another striking feature of these studies is that note is taken not just of musical episodes themselves but of the surrounding activity and context. Moorhead and Pond propose that 'chants', for instance, appear in connection with social group activity, often started by one child and taken up by the group. They are accompanied by 'continued physical activity involving the large muscles in rhythmic movement' (ibid.: 11) or arise following 'large constructive activity', prolonged musical experience or in association with a celebration of some kind. Analysis of the verbal forms of chants is given showing how they emerge from rhythmic speech patterns, rhymes, and play with words (ibid.: 13).

Pond and Moorhead found children's musical activity so bound up with movement and speech that they widened their observations to try to 'learn how and when they assumed musical importance'. They outline in detail the way music grows in rhythmic interest as the movement vocabulary expands:

> He uses instruments while he is moving or after he has been moving; he grows able to abstract his movement rhythms into pure sound. In particular he seems to feel the typical movement sensation of running to a sudden stop, slide or jump. Many of his early instrumental rhythms are of this kind. He makes vocal sounds similar in character – a 'scoop' upwards with a long *portamento* fall, or a rapid series of repeated syllables culminating in a cry. These rhythmic patterns themselves become subjects for experiment. He subjects them to augmentation and diminution, to extension and contraction.
>
> (Moorhead and Pond 1942: 40)

Observing children's music in the context of movement work or outdoor play opens up another realm, with its own characteristic features. A further interesting point is made concerning songs children are taught to sing.

> The greater number of the songs which young children usually are taught to sing are in all ways unlike their own music. They are based upon a measured concept of rhythm, while the child's are free and *senza misura*.

They are always inevitably in major or (less frequently) minor tonality and usually refer to a harmonic system dominated by the tonic, dominant and sub-dominant harmonies of the diatonic harmonic system. The child's natural songs are melodic, do not belong necessarily to diatonic or any other tonality and refer to no harmonic system; they may be modal or atonal, and are non-harmonic. The words of most songs that are taught to children are infrequently imaginative and are often doggerel or composed in pedestrian verse forms. Nothing is more noticeable than the contrast between the energetic, bright tone of the songs that young children are made to sing and the plaintive quality of the songs that they sing for themselves.

(Moorhead and Pond 1942: 42)

This raises major questions about the kind of music we introduce for children to sing or listen to. How does it, and how far should it, connect with the music they produce? The music made available for listening at the Pillsbury Foundation school was drawn from across many different world traditions, another respect in which this work might retrospectively be seen as far ahead of its time.

In summary, some of the main points emerging from the work of Moorhead and Pond are as follows.

- Musical activity and learning are inseparable from other learning.
- 'To study the music of the young child one must consider not only such music as adults arbitrarily decide to recognise, but must observe all musical beginnings which are to combine to become that music.'
- Song is essentially produced by the child for himself. Whereas the form of chants remains fixed, songs change and assume personal characteristics.
- The child's first interest with musical instruments is timbre – sound making, trying different surfaces, sticks, ways of beating, repeating and listening; dynamics too might be heard as another way of varying sound.
- Rhythmic order is first accent within a series of beats, often irregular.
- Rhythms may be asymmetrical and structured in relation to pulse; later rhythmic motifs appear.
- Embryonic composition techniques:

    Of the following we have enough examples to make us believe that their occurrence is not fortuitous: rhythmic variation, vocal and instrumental; sequential progression; adaptations of rhythmic passages to verbal forms and vice versa; rhythmic counterpoint; melodic and rhythmic augmentation and diminution; antiphony; recurrent refrains – a primitive rondo form; instrumentation especially in group performances; transference of a rhythm from one instrument to another.

    (Moorhead and Pond 1942: 47)

- The pattern of the child's life, with its musical incidents, will often contain during one activity musical forms which appear (different only in their degree of sophistication) in dramatic music of all times – arias, recitatives, choruses, solos with choral interludes etc. (ibid.: 47).

What comes across most strongly from these studies is the sense of young children's music having its own characteristic features and not simply being a pale or incompetent imitation of the adult world around them. The holistic and wide-ranging nature of these studies enters territory which more recent research has only partially begun to open up again (Foley 1978; Shelley 1996), hampered as it has been by restrictive approaches to research methodologies. At the very least, it offers teachers a rich and intriguing set of observations to draw on in listening to children's music-making in their own classrooms.

Observation in play settings is one of the most useful sources of information for the teacher in establishing baselines from which to plan for music learning. The dearth of research in naturalistic settings means that there is little available to help teachers with even broad indications of what to look for or expect. In a study of the influence of play settings on pre-school (4–5 year old) children's music and play behaviours, Littleton (1991) notes this and suggests that pedagogic practice that does not allow time for free play in music raises questions of developmental appropriateness. She also recommends some preparation of teachers as observers of musical behaviours in the free play environment.

Littleton's study is useful in making comparisons between children's participation in 'music specific' and 'non-music' play settings; in this case 'house play' with dressing up clothes, pots and pans and so on. Looking at social, cognitive and musical play behaviours in both types of settings, she found that 'socially, the music setting engendered nearly twice as much solitary play than did the house play setting while both settings encouraged group play'. She also found that 'a strong preference for instrumental musical play [as opposed to vocal or movement play] was exhibited by boys and girls in the music setting', whereas 'when music play occurred in the house setting, girls showed a preference for movement, and boys demonstrated vocal and instrumental behaviours'. Her observations include some quite long episodes of musical play. For example, one child's 'first encounter with the Chinese gong resulted in a solitary play episode for nearly thirty minutes in one session, and resumed similarly in the following four music play episodes' (Littleton 1991: 168). This bears out the experience of many that young children have considerable powers of sustaining work and concentration in their musical activities.

Patterns and structures in children's music-making

The essence of the music created freely and in play situations is that it is made as played or made as sung. The delight for the listener in following the music lies both in the small patternings and in the life and character of the music as a whole, changing as it does from moment to moment. If it is to be analysed, rather than just experienced holistically, then it is best thought of in terms of dramatic form rather than architectural form. In this sense, the music is an experience of lived time and not of a construction.

In listening to the music that arises as part of young children's play, it can be helpful to approach it from several different perspectives. The first, and perhaps most important of all, is to simply listen-in and be carried along by the music as a whole, entering into the spirit in which it is made. Listening to the musical stream and just following it, without expectations of clear cut outcomes, is the easiest way to tap into our own musical responses and enjoy the energy and imagination in the music. Another way of listening is to try to hear the music through whatever observable factors are driving it – movement, drama, mood or the physical, visual or other contextual factors that might be playing a part. T's drum music (page 51) was compelling to watch as well as listen to, since the music was determined by his tapping all the way round the edge of the drum head until he got back to the beginning. Then he struck the drum hard in the middle. The two different timbres held his attention and he found the circular pathway a very satisfying way to use the circular instrument. Somehow the visual context affects how we hear this music, which would lose some of its tension if heard only as an indefinite stream of drum beats.

If listening is to be more analytical, getting inside the way the music is structured, then an important key to most young children's music is to listen for the small-scale structures before the larger ones. As a listening adult, it is a mistake to approach children's spontaneous music as if it were a constructed whole, unless there are clear indications that this is so. The structures of music arising spontaneously as part of children's play or other activity can be heard at three levels:

1   There will be a very rich variety of small-scale patternings; these constitute the main musical organisation.
2   There will be a middle level of structuring arising from repetitions and transformations of patterns or from sequences of new pattern ideas appearing as the music goes on.
3   There may be some overall 'form' to a musical episode or event, although it is likely to be fairly loose or vague; songs are more likely to have an overall shape than instrumental music.

Of these, the first is where the most 'intentional' music-making is found, if considered in terms of children's purposeful inventiveness and exploration. This is also where the music is often at its richest as patterns are found in so many ways, and often have a strength, appeal and also subtlety not unlike the richness of colour, pattern and shape in children's art work. Some common forms of patterning are:

•   patterns of timbre, the different sound qualities produced by voice or instrument (for example, R's music for tambour)

Figure 4.2 Early years rhythm pieces

- patterns of dynamics, louder and softer sounds, accent and silence (K, playing with M)
- patterns of number, often mixtures such as twos and threes (P's glockenspiel music in which the number of pitches changes between the 'glissando' – slide – each time)
- patterns of rhythm, longer and shorter sounds, accents and movement, with

or without a basic pulse (J, M and Q working with regular or irregular rhythms over a pulse, or P working without a pulse but using rhythmic movement)

• patterns of melody, tune patterns of different pitches, slides and decorations, perhaps in phrases of different lengths (M, patterning over a rhythmic tambourine line).

Examples of these can be seen on page 51.

These are, of course, the fundamental structurings of most music and the fact that they are only loosely structured at the second and third levels (shown earlier) should not detract from their musical value at the heart of children's work.

Patterns carry musical expressiveness and their infinite variety enables music to take on all shades of character. They can be heard in an abstract way, offering purely the aesthetic satisfaction of pattern itself. Or they can be heard dramatically, colouring the music as it takes its course over time. It is at the level of such patternings that children first become aware of their own musical thinking. Patterns may be remembered, returned to, copied, played with and transformed. A teacher can investigate children's patternings with them by learning and copying or describing them in words. Children can be helped to make musical patterns visible, by drawing them on paper or in sand, or using stones, shells or any other flexible materials to 'show' the pattern or even to record and save it.

Adults listening to musical play

Teachers, parents and carers can share in children's music play, just as they can in other play situations. This may be by invitation to participate, or it may arise from just being alongside the child playing. Being a listener, giving quiet and companionable attention without intervening can be a real contribution in musical terms. This may simply give support and encouragement or it may introduce the audience factor, with the possibilities of communication or making an impact. From the teaching point of view, a listening role which may move in and out of interactive musical participation has particularly rich potential. Being listened to, however briefly, helps the child to listen to what they are doing as well as do it. Joining in and making music alongside or in turns has direct parallels with the ways in which adults encourage children's language development by talking to them. Similar strategies of accommodation, extending and 'scaffolding' can be introduced. In this kind of play partnering, cues from the child enable the adult to know whether they are 'in tune' with the child's musical focus and understanding.

It is also important to realise that this is a part of the ground on which the child's music becomes mediated and understood within the wider, adult world. Adult to child interactions are a crucial part of this process. These may take the form of the adult listening followed by verbal response and discussion.

More immediately, musical interaction – playing or singing together – opens up the opportunity for musical understanding to develop within the untranslatable but social context of musical communication itself. Arguably, this kind of interactive play with music should be the central mainstay of work with children in the early years. At best, it will happen freely and fluidly at any time of day as an ordinary part of classroom life. In this way, music-making takes its place as a social and expressive medium alongside language. For most young children, this is quite naturally connected to the way they move in and out of musical behaviour anyway.

Young draws on the idea of music as an expressive medium for making and sustaining relationships to suggest a continuum which extends from the 'micro-music world' of early infant communication with care-givers into the musical activity of three and four year olds and on into adulthood. In a study of inter-personal features of spontaneous music-play on instruments among nursery aged children, she concludes:

> Theorists suggest that language emerges from an interpersonal basis (e.g. Bruner 1990), not only as a model and support to children's learning but that the actual structures of language are embedded in pre-verbal exchanges with adults. Similarly I propose that essentials of music, its fundamental parameters of time, space and energy, its use as an expressive medium for relating self to others and its structuring of time, can be conceived as evolving out of a dynamic system of interactions between child and adult involved in dyadic music play with instruments.
>
> Young (1999)

By comparing time spent playing instruments, with and without an adult present, Young found that the quantity of music play was increased by the presence of an interested, attendant adult. In addition, the interpersonal context encouraged functional play actions to become fused with expressive intent. She also links the presence of an adult 'play partner' to an increase in the child's sense of musical intention. This happens through bringing into play a temporal sense of past and future with predictive elements that are lacking when children play alone. These findings endorse the potential value of adults making music with young children. In addition to any general benefits, they suggest that music learning is enhanced, particular in relation to children's awareness of and purposes for their own music.

If this is so, music-making with an adult becomes a third dimension for children's musical play, alongside making music alone and making music with other children. As with the role parents, teachers and other adults take in language development, we need to acknowledge the role that interactive and communicative activity with adults can have in children's musical development. Adult partnering is surprisingly little used as a conscious methodology in music learning situations; yet all teachers of young children have a sophisticated understanding of the importance of adult linguistic interaction for children's development. Both are extensions of behaviour which comes relatively easily to parents and caregivers. Once in school, however, the process in music teaching is more likely to be one of 'listen and copy' with the child making most of the accommodations.

The teacher's role in relation to early years music-making may be summarised as that of:

- providing a rich environment for music-making, including a variety of instruments of different timbres and structures
- making opportunities for free, uninterrupted music play
- listening to emergent music-making to gain understanding of its musical qualities
- offering play partnering, listening or participating
- introducing discussion and vocabulary as part of the first moves towards metacognition
- helping children recognise small-scale patternings, perhaps showing these visually
- beginning to make links between children's musical ideas and those found in other music.

If teachers can go at least halfway towards meeting children on their own musical ground, and can begin to listen, join in with and talk about music-making together with children, they can help children to begin to understand their music-making in relation to the music of others. Gradually, children start to gain awareness of their own music, of how it sounds and feels, and of how they can control and shape musical materials towards their own musical purposes.

Chapter 5

Composing

The watershed

Around the age of 6 or 7, children cross a watershed in their musical thinking that brings a new possibility into play in terms of music-making. This is the point at which they become able not just to make, but to think of, musical 'pieces' as such. The realisation comes that the music they create has its own existence, as apart from the activity of making it. The music can be listened to, sung or played by others, captured and kept, and revisited at any time.

In the period leading up to this point, children invent songs and tunes and instrumental pieces with beginnings and endings, particularly in their vocal music-making. These are their earliest compositions. Often these pieces emerge from a stream of musical 'thinking aloud', in what is essentially a development of the musical play activity described in the previous chapter. Gradually they become able to conceptualise, and operate with, the idea of musical structures as having shape and identity. The consequence of this new thinking is that the activity of composing, in its traditional sense, becomes fully available and begins to separate from the activity of improvising. Composing becomes inclusive not only of purpose and intention in music-making, which has been there from very early on, but of the idea of an end product with its own character and impact. Children become able to work on their compositions in stages comparable to the processes of writing: drafting, editing, saving and finally 'publishing', that is, performing their work. When R announces 'that was my composement', after playing a piece she's composed for piano (p.77), she uses a common grammatical construction for turning verbs into nouns. This reflects just what is happening creatively. By 8 years old, the activity of composing leads quite definitely to a 'composement'. This represents a significant developmental shift.

This is not to suggest, however, that improvised music, made as sung or played, becomes any less important within the whole spectrum of children's music-making. The development of improvising skills continues as an important part of musical creativity, and improvising continues to have a reciprocal and complex relationship with composing throughout the age-phase covered in this book. This is a topic that has interested researchers (Burnard 1999a) and to which discussion returns in later chapters. Composing and improvising become related but distinguishable activities alongside children's performing, as all three begin to take on more of the role boundaries that they hold in the adult cultures in which children grow up. These roles in themselves shift in relation to different musical cultures and even styles, some pieces being almost entirely improvisation-based, others composition based, entailing different expectations of performers. Maintaining some fluidity between the three strands of music-making is important for the vitality of each. Exploring the boundaries with pupils can be stimulating and interesting in itself.

This chapter looks at ways of working with children's music-making during the period leading up to this watershed. Between 5 and 7 years old, children are learning fast in almost all areas and music is no exception. The range of maturity even within one class can be wide and the distance travelled during a school year is considerable. Moreover, things do not happen at an even pace. All learning tends to alternate between spurts of progress and quieter periods of consolidation. Some of the most important groundwork for later composing can be done during this age-phase but the learning benefits are not always directly or immediately perceptible.

Just before the end of the first term with a reception class (rising 5s), a teacher writes:

> Suddenly they are composing on the spot, re-inventing, and above all developing what one of them has started, as a *class*, not just in twos and threes. They invent songs, and another group puts in a counter rhythm. Of course it helps to have two or three leaders/naturals, but the others follow. They listen to a rhythm, and try to decide the beat: introducing 'ta-te' [a system of naming time-values] has been easy and instant. They listen to a rhythm and put words to it. They won't stop! Jam sessions go on for twenty minutes, when really I had planned to discuss maths.
>
> I think early symbolisation may be good – if their auditory memory is still partial, then a visual record is surely going to help, particularly as they move on to more sustained composition and planned structure. They still bed down in a corner with the music box and play away – some lovely things and I suppose some new ways of friendship too. So perhaps it won't stifle them to be organised quite rigorously at times.
>
> A new development is teaching them in turn to conduct the class as an orchestra. Oh, the power! Better than a drum! And the discipline from the orchestra. . . .
>
> What makes it most exciting is I was beginning to think nothing was working. The extraordinary thing is that it really did happen overnight.
>
> (my italics)

Of course, it does and it doesn't happen overnight. Behind the leap forward into a new stage – in this case, the move into improvising music together as a class – lie daily small activities: focusing listening, learning songs, modelling composing ideas, introducing vocabulary and ways of talking. The key to sustaining young children's musical liveliness is in creating a rich and vibrant environment, with a flow of small inputs and different ways of approaching music, constantly responding to and building on the children's own work as their abilities develop. What is evident from the above description is how the teacher's offered provision is balanced by a readiness to take the moment, when the moment arises, and allow the music the children generate to lift off too. This is skilful teaching, but it is based on very small amounts of time – music in the cracks of the day almost – used imaginatively in maintaining consistent interest. It is also interactive, with skills and understanding brought reciprocally to extend the children's ideas and discoveries.

For this age group particularly, the secret of success in fostering children's improvisations and compositions is for the teacher to let go of the expectation of a tight and immediate connection between what might crudely be termed 'input' and 'output'. The quality of children's own music-making is undoubtedly at its highest when the opportunity for it is relatively free from direction. Paradoxically, once given this freedom, children both can and do draw extensively on other recent musical experiences, in school and beyond. The teacher's role is crucial, however, in providing for stimulating and appropriate musical experiences, and developing skills, understanding, and ways of thinking and talking about music. Unforced, these are readily drawn into the individual child's own work, where motivation is also at its highest to experiment, practise and to gain better control and understanding. In turn, this gives the listening teacher a sharper insight into the child's capabilities and learning needs, so that future inputs can be well matched and challenging.

Such an approach is far more effective than the introduction of a musical idea – for example, contrasting louder and quieter sounds – followed by the immediate requirement to 'make a piece using louder and quieter sounds'. Something may well be produced, but the listener will immediately be able to tell the difference between these exercises and the quality of children's 'real' music. Furthermore, the ideas introduced, as in this example, may be far more simplistic than those which have been used in the child's own music-making for months or years. So the musical level of the work drops like a stone. This can set off a spiral of lowering expectation, if the teacher finds the outcomes disappointing and imagines that the ideas are too difficult for the children to take on board. In early years music, it is often *how* ideas are introduced that is so crucial, together with right timing. In this instance, the conceptual tool – sounds may be louder or quieter – is meaningless without a musical context in which the subtlest of dynamic gradations or the wildest of contrasts are used towards a felt musical intention. It is difficult for children of this age, or for any of us for that matter, to accommodate to the challenge set without losing a sense of meaningful musical direction. If, in addition, they are trying to do so in a group or class, it becomes almost impossible for them to do more than construct, rather as they build with Lego. Such constructions may have a role in demonstrating possibilities, but they cannot be seen as substitutes for children making their own music.

From the teacher's point of view, then, it is useful to see work in music with this age group in two ways and provide concurrently:

- a wide range of music-making opportunities for individual or paired work
- a wide range of teacher led experiences, in the form of both input and classwork.

These two areas of experience can then be allowed to link together and inform each other through the child's own activity. The connections that arise can also be made explicit by the teacher once they are part of the children's own experience. This enables understanding to stretch further and conforms better to children's own ways of learning. Gradually children's awareness of what they are doing and hearing grows and teachers can foster this metacognition. By and large, children soak up the music around them faster than we'd ever imagine. A song introduced to a small group at break time is known by everyone by the time they go home.

Integrating music in the early years curriculum

One of the strongest aids for the early years teacher working with musical improvisation and composition is music's intrinsic connectedness with other fundamental areas of learning. Music and language, music and mathematics, and music and movement share common ground at a deep human level. For young children, allowing these alliances to remain intact and working with them enables learning to be enriched all round and does no more than conform to the ways in which their music arises naturally. Word patterning, number patterning and movement patterning are amongst the most fundamental structures emerging in children's music. At a more holistic level, in the feeling for music as song, the interplay between words, meaning, voice timbre, rhythm and melodic shape create more than the sum of the parts. The same interplay can be found in the feeling for music as movement, or movement as music, and with the sense of music as audible number, patterning, sequence and time. Although intuitive for children of this age, and beyond their powers to articulate, these relationships are an audible force in their music. Conversely, pupils can develop their understanding in these other disciplines through the medium of music. This is not a point about superficial curriculum links such as adding sound effects in a story or singing a number song. The resonances reach to the heart of how musical essentially is.

Children's improvised and composed rhymes, chants, dialogues and songs can find a place in the curriculum alongside every other form of language use with which they work: story, conversation, poetry and drama. Music made with or for movement can be a normal part of dance or 'hall time' activity. Scientific investigation of sound, or designing and making instruments,can be extended into instrumental composing. Any vocal or instrumental music children have made can be investigated to allow its mathematical magic to appear. A number strategy can often be explored in sound, just as well as in visual and tactile materials. In addition music can be made for all the events, daily purposes, and special occasions that thread through the year. And it can be made simply to be listened to: as a live performance for the class gathered instead of a story, to be played or sung for a group of friends, or recorded for independent listening on headphones in the classroom.

The first tune (a) on page 60 was made on a chromatic glockenspiel and brought by L (age 6) for a group to listen to. Played rather slowly to begin with, it held the children's attention with its spacious quality and unfamiliar note set. L almost seemed to breathe with each phrase. Although she could repeat the tune, it seemed probable that the precise pitches were less the focus of her attention than the phrase structure and shapes. Thinking, listening and watching, the children latched quickly on to the pattern of threes and fives that gives the number shape so clear in this music. Discussion was aided by showing these patterns with stones and shells, using a one-to-one correspondence, and shadowing with hand and arm movements whether the phrase went generally upwards or downwards. The fundamental concepts are simple and audible, including threeness, fiveness, repeating, adding or extending, reversing (up then down), and 'same but different' (pitch–shape–number). There was plenty of scope to be analytical and also hypothetical (for example, by asking questions such as: 'what if she . . . ?). But throughout the short session there was also the sense of the music's own quality as the compelling force. And in this force, in the aesthetic quality of the music, the sound and the number principles operating are one and the same. One piece of music can never be replaced with another with the assumption that it will do the same 'work'. Staying with this tune, even quite briefly, it was clear that the children understood both the workings and the very particular effect of these structures together in the music. It was easy then to abstract the idea that when people make tunes they can think about and feel these different lengths and shapes.

At a more practical level, if we are serious about expecting good composing work from young children they must have plenty of opportunity to work alone. There is no replacement for the ways individual work enables children to develop their music and skills. Work in pairs, or other small groupings convened for the occasion, contributes differently by opening up extra inter-active possibilities. While whole class events are exciting catalysts, children need to direct their own music-making and to hear and develop the music as they make it. Providing these different opportunities entails a more flexible approach than confining music to the whole class music lesson. Ideally individual music work sessions will also be of flexible time length and without interruption. Children's concentration can last much longer than generally assumed once they are absorbed in a task. One of the most damaging features of many classrooms is the constant interruption of work, chopping it up into

Figure 5.1 Glockenspiel and xylophone tunes

small pieces. It is also important to acknowledge that the medium of music is sound and to think through the management of the differing sound levels of different musical activities. Above all, work in music demands quiet, quality time and space, not easy to provide in schools. It should not evoke the horrors of a perpetual free-for-all music table piled with tattered instruments and competing noisily with other classroom activity.

Talking about music

As children become increasingly aware of their own composing activity, the teacher can reinforce and build on this. This can even start with some thoughtful discussion about what composing is at all. How *is* music made? What do you do when you're making it up? Where do the musical ideas come from? These are questions which even quite young children can become interested in thinking about. Asking 6 and 7 year olds what a composer is can elicit answers ranging from 'a thing that records music' to 'someone who makes music' or 'a really famous music teacher'. Perceptions of what is involved may be very practical: 'the composer has to play the music too'; 'they'd write the song down and then they'd play it and try it out'; 'they'd go and buy some instruments that they think are jazzy and they'd just play around with them until they'd made up a good tune'; 'they actually write it down and then if you have a special computer that only types out notes, they might type it out on the computer'. Or they may lead into consideration of the process of getting ideas: 'she got out of her house and looked for what she was going to write about', 'they have to think hard before they write it, otherwise it goes out of tune and they play the wrong note'.

This kind of discussion also reveals the kinds of models children are drawing on, ranging across musical styles, processes involving notation or not, and including images absorbed from different media such as cartoons, books and television: 'they look smart and a bit like a butler'. Reflection on how other people compose help children consider how they might do it.

A major part of the teacher's role in encouraging talk about music is to model it. This can begin with listening and reflecting back to children what they have done in their own music, as described in Chapter 3. Distinguishing different ways of talking about music begins to be important at this stage for both teacher and pupils (Young and Glover 1998). It is particularly useful to be aware of the distinction between giving feedback that names, describes or analyses the musical features or structure, and discussing subjective responses. Both have value but the differences should be clear. As developing composers, children need to acquire an understanding of how music works *musically*, so that they can build a repertoire of techniques that can be used towards their intended effect. However, they also need to increase their experience of how such techniques produce musical effect and to listen and decide on the aesthetic result that they want. Inside this process is a sensitivity to musical materials in themselves, to the timbres of sound, to rhythm, melody, texture and so on. Here it is important to realise that music affects people differently and that they must trust their own judgements. On this ground, it is helpful for teachers and other children to describe their own responses to the music, fostering the understanding that we will all hear it differently. This is a quite different kind of discussion. So it may be useful to be clear about the following kinds of talk about music with children, which teachers can be modelling:

- naming musical features: introducing vocabulary relating to musical elements such as *rhythm pattern, steady beat, getting louder, melody shape*; or musical techniques, for example, *two tunes keeping together*; or singing or playing techniques such as *scraping and tapping the drum, sliding up with your voice*
- describing what happens in the music, in musical terms: for example. 'first we heard . . . ', 'just before the end the jumpy rhythm got louder'
- describing the form of the music: 'the music gradually built up', 'it stopped and started again twice; it was in two sections'
- picking out noticeable characteristics: 'the two ways of playing the tambourine were mixed in all the way through', 'the music went suddenly high, but came lower slowly'
- analysing some aspect of the music: 'the second pattern started the same but went different; the first pattern kept coming back';

and

- describing how the music affects me (using first person)
- describing what it reminds me of (musically, or otherwise)
- making an evaluation of how the music 'works' in its own terms.

It can also be useful to increase children's awareness of their own music by questioning. In this case, it is better to keep a similar distinction between different kinds of talk. The question 'How could you make the music better?' is not a good starting point. Not only does this ride roughshod over the principle of focusing on what the children *have* done in their music, as opposed to what they haven't done, but it also distracts attention from taking on board the impact of the music as it is. For young children, once finished the music is made. To 'do it differently' is to make some new music. It will be more helpful to ask very open questions, such as 'can you tell me about your music?'. Alternatively, questions can be made along the lines of the types of descriptive talk given earlier: 'how did the music begin?', 'what did you most notice about your music?', 'how can you describe the rhythm pattern?'. The conversation can be scaffolded, with the teacher supplying vocabulary and language which supports the child's train of thought. This enables discussion to reflect the focus of the child's musical interest, whether this stems from the words in a song, or the patternings on an instrument. It also aids awareness of which musical elements are predominant in the making process: words, timbre and dynamics, rhythm, pitch and melody. Moog (1976) shows how children's awareness and interest as listeners is differently focused on musical elements during the early years of development. The same shifts of perception are evident in their music-making, following more or less the sequence here. The teaching function of holding a mirror up to the music made, encouraging children to look at and listen to their music and to begin to recognise and describe its musical features, is of key importance for this age group. To do this without shattering the magic of the music, as listened to and felt, is not easy, but with sensitive timing both understanding and musical responsiveness can be increased together. Little by little, by catching the moment, children's awareness of what they're doing and the impact of their music on themselves and others as listeners is absorbed back into the making process.

The following sections look at the twofold teaching process of providing opportunities for children to make music and of building on what they do, matching inputs with current levels of skill and understanding. For both practical and developmental reasons, vocal and instrumental music are discussed separately, although in reality they do share some common ground.

Making music with voices

Children's spontaneous music-making shows how inventive and full of life their vocal improvisations and songs are from an early age. This is a natural form of behaviour for young children and can readily be encouraged and developed in school. In addition, most children have been singing and listening to songs from an early age, so that song-making relates easily to the rest of their musical experience (see Chapter 2).

Song and story are fundamental and familiar forms of language use. For children, hearing these and making their own are easily related activities. In a wider context, learning what voices can do, and that all our voices are different, helps to develop imagination, skills and confidence for children as singers and speakers. Exploring the different possibilities in the human voice enriches the fund of aural images children can draw on in later composing. These might include whispering, humming, short staccato sounds, and wordless pitch shapes, as well as many different voice timbres and dynamics. The New York composer Meredith Monk talks about the role of the voice in her music:

> I start with my own voice, and always have. . . . I start with my own instrument and explore the parameters of that world. This is how I began as a soloist. But when you work with all the different possibilities of your own instrument, you do come upon things that exist in a lot of different cultures that are trans-cultural. In a sense, you become part of the world

vocal family. There's something very comforting about that, because it is being part of something that has always existed and always will exist. Of course, each of our voices is totally unique. You might have a set of vocal sound possibilities that I might not be able to do or which wouldn't be comfortable for me, and I would have different ones that might not be comfortable for you. Our vocal mechanisms are totally unique. Also, in all cultures there are what I would call archetypal songs – the lullaby form, work song, love song, march, funeral song. It's interesting to hook into these song categories that exist all over.

(Smith and Walker Smith 1994: 190–1)

Making opportunities for improvising and composing songs is relatively straightforward, needing no instruments other than the voice children have with them all the time. At most, this might be supported by recording equipment for saving the music or the materials for making simple notations. Children working alone can sing quietly to themselves or into a tape or minidisc recorder. Class times can be organised when a few minutes can be found and without elaborate preparation, perhaps at the end of a story or circle time. A well-known story may itself supply song opportunities, particularly a story with a repeating structure or clear group or individual characters. One child can make a song for a particular part of the story and the next for another. These may be improvised or more considered and composed.

Song-making can be introduced in class as a spontaneous improvisation activity. A useful framework for this is to ask: 'Would anyone like to sing us a song?'. Hands go up and the class can listen to two or three singers. This question in itself may produce an invented song, but it is more likely that children will choose known songs. This makes a good lead into the follow-up question 'Would anyone like to make us a song?' or 'a new song' or 'a song of their own'? The group can listen and songs can be just enjoyed for themselves or lead into some discussion, as above. Links might be made to other songs the class sing by noticing common features such as a verse structure, a repeating rhythm, a melody shape or an ending idea. If the song is short and simple enough, the group can learn it and it joins the class repertoire.

S, aged 6, prefaced her song offering by saying 'I know a song!' just as the idea for one came into her head. The improvised music (see page 65) is an example of the kind of narrative song often produced by children at this stage. The story provides a framework on which the song can be built. Yet there is a clear sense that the child has grasped, albeit intuitively, how songs demand some kind of agreement between words and rhythm. As the song is sung, the struggle to accommodate the two is almost audible. In the one line where the words go off the end in relation to the musical structure, at ' she didn't know where it was', S gives the story priority but quickly resumes the rhythmic patterning. In the final line there isn't enough story so an extra word, 'after' is added to fit with the music in bringing the song to a close. A teacher listening can hear the extent to which the child

One day I was going down the street, and I saw my friend and she saw a witch and I saw her too, and (swallow) we both ran to our house and our mother came with us and we saw that witch a-gain. So we ran back to our house and she did-n't know where it was and she ne-ver went with, af-ter us a-gain.

Figure 5.2 Song: 'One day I was going down the street'

Source: Glover and Ward 1998: 142

has absorbed features of how songs 'go', particularly here the way each phrase ends with a longer and accented note, and the new section which begins halfway through.

Davies finds that children's songs of this narrative type tend to have more of the character of 'rudimentary chants' than other songs produced. Melodies often have a narrow pitch range and are delivered in a kind of 'sing-song' manner suggesting that attention is mainly on the words. S's song is of this kind, with its melody centred on a recurring falling figure. Davies comments:

> Many of these narrative songs do contain more developed musical ideas. Sometimes this is a stringing together of apparently unrelated figures; but many songs use a repeated figure, and perhaps focus on one or two notes as 'home' notes. This seems to suggest that children are 'practising tonicity'. It also suggests an increasing ability to embody the verbal content with musical ideas, and calls to mind the way in which plainchant uses repetition rather than contrast or development to carry the words. Often though, the children vary the repeated figure, usually at the end, sometimes at the middle cadence as well, which suggests an awareness of closure and the way in which it may be indicated.
>
> (Davies 1992: 25)

Once established, song making opportunities usually produce far more songs than there is really time for, and back-up strategies may be needed, such as singing your song to a friend or onto a tape recorder. There might be an understanding that any of the adults in the class, teachers or assistants, is always interested to hear children's made-up songs. This is simply offering a listening ear. As above, it has dangers of escalation and excessive demands being made on the attention that can be given. But to see this alongside listening to something a child wants to tell the teacher is simply a matter of acknowledging song singing as a valid form of communication. 'Sing me a song of yours' can be a one-to-one affair, just a brief moment. In fact, some children who won't speak will sing.

Song-making opportunities may arise to meet a purpose. In this case, the words will often be found first and rhythm and tune sought out later. Again, a general appeal might be made: 'Who could make us some words for a 'waiting to go' song?' followed by 'Could you find a tune for the words that we could all sing?'. These songs may be short – one or two liners – but are very good for singing together and for modelling the idea that if you need a song you just make one. Some children, particularly towards the older end of this age group, will enjoy working on composing a song for a time before bringing it for others to listen to. Children remember songs quite easily and the words help to give a secure reminder of rhythm and even tune. Memorable songs can be collected as an anthology, with an invitation for anyone to contribute a song.

Some indication of the potential for young children's song making is shown by research carried out by Davies into songs invented by children aged 5–7 years. Working with groups ranging from eight to sixteen children in a weekly singing session over eighteen months, Davies followed a mixed programme of singing familiar songs, learning new ones and playing singing and dancing games. From this context, she asked children to make their own songs too.

> I would invite children to sing their own made-up songs, which almost every child was very willing to do. Sometimes we made a song together, with children volunteering lines that I then sang back to them; in this way we could build up something to sing together. Sometimes I offered a starter, to words or 'lah'. Occasionally songs were offered, and recorded, in the playground or corridor as 'inspiration' prompted.
>
> (Davies 1992: 24)

Davies' study contains detailed observation and analysis of the musical means these children were able to bring to achieving their expressive purposes across a range of different song types. Davies highlights some widespread features of these children's songs, in particular the use of closure devices such as a falling phrase or repeated notes and of the four-phrase structure so frequently found in the songs they sing. This is supported by Barrett's findings, from a similarly extensive study of children's vocal and instrumental compositions (1996), that children of this age-group are able to develop musical ideas structurally as a means to realising their musical purposes. Davies also presents several examples of series of work produced by individual children. Seeing a child's work as a developing collection in this way is crucial in encouraging composing to move forward and not just remain as an occasional activity without learning expectations. Davies' accounts show how much children will drive their own development forward if allowed the space to do it. Her account of one child's work, C, includes the following learning sequence:

> 2 songs based on a borrowed standard song, both about a squirrel; applying a similar underlying structure to produce two versions.
>
> Using similar framework but making a completely new song with a very personal story about her lost kitten.
>
> Making long story songs and making wordless songs that structure purely melodic ideas.
>
> Taking written words to use for songs; singing A. A. Milne poems to the tune of *Twinkle Twinkle Little Star*; 'practising modifying words or tune to accommodate'.
>
> Using a formula for words (ab bb ab c) which other children copied.
>
> Continuing story songs and short four-line pieces, with and without words.
>
> Trying to remember her songs. Carrying work across sessions using a borrowed tune.
>
> (Researcher suggests making a new tune).
>
> Beginning to remember newly made music of her own.
>
> (paraphrased)

Several of these ideas were taken up by other children. This is characteristic of how composing ideas can escalate once music-making is under way in a context in which children's work is both owned by individuals and shared with the class.

Making music with instruments

For children under 7, most instrumental music-making will be based on exploratory work with a whole range of different instruments. In addition, some children will be beginning to acquire some technical playing skills on instruments for which they have tuition. For all instrumental work, it is essential that children have the time and opportunity to practise with instruments if their work is to become skilful. At this stage, improvising and composing are wholly dependent on the skills of producing sounds from the instrument. Trying out new techniques, exploring sound quality, listening to oneself play, repeating over and over, building up new musical ideas and revisiting music made before all require time alone. Taking a turn with an instrument now and again in a music lesson isn't enough. Some arrangement is needed for independent work: a music work-base inside or just outside the classroom, or a music box or cupboard from which equipment is borrowed. The quietest situation and some degree of permanence is best. One at a time can be the norm with exceptions for paired or group work as the need arises. Instruments can be introduced in turn in whole class sessions and then made available for independent work later, gradually building up the range of experiences on offer. It is often better to provide fewer instruments rather than more, with the arrangement that particular instruments can be asked for if required. At times selections can be classified for additional focus, for example, wood, metal or string instruments.

Any instrument suggests its own musical structures. The musical patternings young children make with instruments often arise from a response to the visual structure and the action and sound patternings which these suggest (Glynne-Jones 1974). A two-tone woodblock or a pair of bongo drums obviously invite patternings of lower and higher tones. Bongos suggest two-handed playing which results in left and right hand action patternings. A circular drumhead presents the visual opportunity to play in the middle or round the edge. Rattles and shakers immediately reflect not just movement or stillness but very subtle gradations and quality of movement. A child picking up any instrument of this kind is immediately drawn into patterning, not just rhythmically but with timbre, intensity, dynamics and qualities ranging from smooth to staccato. The higher chance element in some less controllable rattles – rain sticks, for instance – draws children into alternately making the sound and then listening. Similarly, instruments with a long sound decay time, such as gongs, cymbals, temple bowls, and metallophones, lead into music based on striking and waiting, or a punctuating role with a song, as well as letting sound accumulate through repeated strikes. A tambourine that can be rattled or struck leads to music based on combinations of these two very different timbres.

Consequently, the range of opportunities for working with different instruments has a profound impact on the range of musical experience children gain. It is important to try to preserve the very high levels of discrimination between different qualities of sound that children have at this age. Each instrument has its own voice, and a range of potential quite distinct from the next. Children are fascinated by this and it is a pity to dull their senses by treating all instruments as if they are interchangeable. If the focus of instrumental work is limited to playing a steady beat, for example, it is easy to fall into the trap of ignoring the enormous differences between a steady beat played on a frame drum, a rattle, and a zither. This is the age phase in which to capitalise on children's sensitivity to sound quality and their interest in it.

In the earlier stages of instrumental music-making, it is timbre, rhythm and dynamics that are the most readily used structural materials, with enormous scope for shaping and patterning. Children respond to what the instruments suggest, finding great satisfaction in sequencing sounds in different ways, each giving back its own aesthetic character for enjoyment. And it may be the kinaesthetic experience of making particular sound patternings that absorbs attention. Children need to accumulate experience of creating sound, of listening and storing sound images in their minds and finding them again, and of controlling the sound production with fine gradations produced by listening and good motor control. This lays the foundations for the knowledge of how instruments behave, aurally and technically, that is essential to later composing.

Pitched percussion instruments or keyboards with notes presented in order – low pitch to high pitch – offer a visual analogue of what is heard and this becomes very important for children in making the transition from random to structured melody making. Comparison of vocal and instrumental melodies made by young children shows how much the instrument used affects the structure produced. Early melodic compositions on wind instruments such as recorders, tin whistles and ocarinas, follow the logic of the different fingering systems. The melodies on page 60 are all made by 6 and 7 year olds on glockenspiels and xylophones, often the first pitched instruments young children encounter. They show something of the ways children approach tune-making at the point at which they are beginning to compose 'pieces'.

a   Discussed on page 59, this is an example of patterning based on number and general pitch directions.
b   N bases his music on a repeating rhythm pattern. Very characteristically, a repeated pitch is used for the figure involving quicker notes, as this is easier to manage technically and gives a satisfying weight to the rhythm as the main feature. This music has a confident squareness about it and it centres around the notes F and F sharp.
c   L's music for glockenspiel arose from playing slowly and letting each note ring. She has time to move across the instrument and has worked with wide intervals, so that both tempo and melodic outline give a spacious effect. The first pattern repeats and turns into a new idea, that of gradually reducing the size of the interval between low and high notes. The pauses come just when the new strategy returns her to the opening idea, which is repeated once more before the closing alternation of two adjacent low notes.
d   This tune alternates a hard striking timbre with a softer, winding shape, extended the second time.
e   Here, S is playing a xylophone on which the lowest note is the C that opens the piece and the highest is the A that starts the second pattern. This melody is organised rhythmically but also sets out to play the whole instrument. Coming up from the bottom twice is then mirrored by coming down from the top twice. This leaves the middle still to play, using B flat instead of B. The pattern leaves the music unfinished however, so a glissando dissolves the tension and the children listening giggle at the sliding sound.
f   By contrast, H is planning music entirely by sound. Starting on the second note of her glockenspiel, she chooses the first and last notes of

this melody aurally, and makes her first phrase open and her second closed.

g   Finally, J's strategy is to make a pattern, repeat it, and then move it higher: the same but different.

Most of this thinking is still fairly intuitive at the time the music is made, but the children are ready and able to notice the patternings that underlie the musical shape and character of their own and others' pieces. Listening and watching the music played back, by the child who made it or a teacher, they can correlate action on the instrument with sound. This, or the use of a visual notation, reinforces the awareness of patterning. If music once made is studied in this way, it is a good idea to finish the session by 'just listening', with eyes closed perhaps, to restore the musical wholeness and absorb the total effect.

When children work in pairs or groups, their instrumental work takes on interactive structures such as turn-taking, joining-in-with, keeping together, following on from, copying, opposing and so on. For children of this age these interactions can be to a degree unreliable. Centred as they still are very much in their own music-making activity, there is some variability in the degree to which they are able to manage their own music at a genuinely interactive level with another player. Music can arise which is genuinely co-operative in intent, but with each player pursuing his or her own musical structuring in parallel to, rather than interaction with, the others. The listener may read this as a jumble; yet careful tracking of each player can reveal very coherent music taking place individually even if it is not yet co-ordinated within the group. At other times, the interaction may be fully there and the musical outcomes can surprise even those taking part, as they feel from the inside the way the music is working together.

Alongside the ideas for music which come from instruments themselves, teachers can be enriching children's fund of musical materials by introducing small inputs focusing on a single musical idea or strategy. These can be modelled by the teacher playing and the children listening, followed by brief discussion and perhaps a link to another musical context, a familiar song, a movement activity, or some listening to recorded music, all centred on the idea being presented. These 'building blocks' (Young and Glover 1998) are offered as small investigations, or in a 'show and say' form, for children to enjoy and absorb. Gradually the ideas can be heard emerging in children's own music as they re-surface during independent exploration. Conversely, an idea that has arisen in a child's music may be taken and presented to the class. Examples of topics might include: comparing the timbres of a percussion instrument played in two differ-ent ways or with different beaters; rhythm patterns made with beats either whole or divided in threes, that is, in compound time ('clackety clack', for instance, or see example e, page 60); moving in thirds, using two sticks on a xylophone; melody shapes played or sung forward or backwards. Listening to examples of music for the instruments children are playing is an essential contribution to widening their awareness of what can be done. Schools may have collections of orchestral music but little music for the pitched or unpitched percussion, pipes, recorders and guitars that children are most likely to be working with in school. Music featuring these in solo or small group contexts enables pupils to relate what they hear to the music they make themselves.

Music in mind

As children move towards the composing watershed, their ability to think musically in their heads increases. The long process of developing the ability to internalise musical sound will be aided by giving encouragement to children to 'think the music' so that this becomes a familiar part of all music-making. Class sessions in which invented songs or instrumental music are listened to can include picking out sounds, patterns or phrases and learning to 'listen to it and then think it'. When children discover new and colourful sounds they can be encouraged to remember them, hearing them again in mind. Children can be asked to think of a musical sound or idea and ask another child to play or sing it. This makes demands on the imagination but also the ability to find words to describe what it envisaged. Thinking a note or phrase and then singing it targets the same skill and games can be used to practise it.

Researchers have been interested in the extent of any correlation for children between abilities in 'audiation' and in composing. This raises complex questions about the extent to which the processes children use when composing, and the balance between working in their heads and working pragmatically with instruments, affect the musical outcomes. Kratus, researching this with 9 year olds, concluded that 'the greater one's ability to audiate, the less one explores while composing' (Kratus 1994: 127). He also found that 'subjects who used greater amounts of exploration created songs (*songs meaning keyboard melodies*) that were less structured and more extensive than did subjects who used less exploration' (ibid.: 127–8). It seems fairly certain, however, that, in the early stages at least, the ability to hear music in our minds is dependent on extensive listening and certainly linked to a wealth of exploratory play with sound. Of course, it does not follow that because a child is exploring with sound she or he is listening to or internalising what is happening, but there is likely to be such an effect.

Another strategy for encouraging children to start thinking about their music in mind is to follow a three stage framework of planning some music-making with the teacher or assistant at the outset, carrying out the plan and then reviewing what has happened in relation to the original plan. This 'plan–do–review' format reinforces the idea of being able to think about what music might be like before making it. It also makes an opportunity to build music vocabulary and language skills and for individuals to use ways of talking about music which help them articulate and develop their own ideas. Saving by recording or notating work (Upitis,1992) can help to establish awareness of what has been made or heard, if the occasion is appropriate. Reviewing work gives an opportunity for playing or singing to other people and describing or evaluating the music itself. It may also be a chance to review skills and identify input or practice that is needed.

The watershed

In *The Arts and Human Development* (1973a), Gardner notes that 'there is an interesting and, I think, important convergence among researchers on the importance of the ages 6–7 in musical development.' Gardner, best known perhaps for his work on multiple intelligences, sees musical intelligence as worthy of consideration as an 'autonomous intellectual realm' (Gardner 1993: 126).

In a much quoted passage he argues

> At least for children with adequate musical potential, it is possible to be a participant in the artistic process by the ages of 5–7. Noteworthy are both the extent to which abilities of the majority of children have unfolded by that age, and the particular capacities of the most talented. . . .
>
> It seems valid to conclude, then, that certain formal properties of music can emerge in the making activity, be noticed by the perceptual systems of children, and involve the feeling system of children at a young age. That is, a reasonably competent 7 year old should understand the basic metrical properties of his musical system and the appropriate scales, harmonies, cadences and groupings, even as he should be able, given some motifs, to combine them into a musical unit that is appropriate for his culture, but is not a complete copy of a work previously known. What is lacking is fluency in motor skills, which will allow accurate performance, experience with the code, tradition and style of that culture, and a range of feeling life. This lack renders children's musical performances and compositions somewhat limited and superficial, even though they are not without charm and spontaneity.
>
> (Gardner 1993: 196–7)

The distinction is made between what is developmentally in place, as it were, by this age and what, through the longer process of skill acquisition and enculturation, will develop on this basis. The major move forward in children's composing coincides with the age by which it appears that the main pieces of the developmental picture are in evidence through children's music-making, perception and responses.

One of the most interesting aspects of children's music in this early phase is that what may be seen as its deficits, as measured in comparison with adult or older children's music, can also be viewed as considerable creative strengths. Much of the work teachers do with older pupils in composition, would be much easier if earlier characteristics could be retained. Examples of this are:

*   the ability to work comfortably in complex rhythm patterns and mixed metres, which simply arise from a holistic sense of patterning

- the ability to invent spontaneously and to play with emerging musical ideas as they gradually transform into kaleidoscopic shape sequences
- the sense of fun with sound, free of stylistic imperatives
- a valuing of the elements of timbre and rhythm.

As children move into the middle years, their music often becomes more convergent on the musical languages most in currency around them. This is, of course, a measure of their growing skills and maturity. If the inventiveness and freedom of the early years can be sustained through the transition into the next stages of composing, their music will benefit from this more divergent thinking.

Chapter 6

Composing pathways

Children aged 8–12

By the age of 8 or so, children are ready to take their own composing forward with a much greater self-awareness than before. They have a new sense of creative ownership of the music they have made and a growing ability to reflect on it objectively. Building on this, a major role for the teacher is to help children gain an ongoing sense of themselves as developing composers. These are the early stages in finding a musical 'voice' that they can recognise as their own.

During the later primary years, or as pupils move from first into middle schools, provision for music may be organised in different ways. Music may be taught by class teachers, each working with their own class across a broad range of curriculum areas, or it may take the form of a weekly lesson with a teacher who takes responsibility for music across the age-range or throughout the school. From the point of view of composing, the class teacher model has the potential for more effective practical provision, although time pressures can prevent this being fully exploited. It allows at least some flexibility of time, and opportunity for individual, paired or group work. It also enables the teacher to make productive cross-curricular links more easily – with language, for example – and it makes the tracking of pupils' accumulating work more straightforward. These possibilities add considerably to the quality of the composing that children do. By contrast, trying to compact all composing work into a short weekly slot, together with the rest of the music curriculum, can be a tall order. As a specialist faced with this model, some liaison with the class teacher is almost essential, particularly for the younger age groups. Once pupils reach the stage at which the whole curriculum is delivered in subject lesson slots by different teachers, other strategies have to be found for the independent work so important to composing development.

Whatever the basis on which music is taught, two factors appear crucial in establishing a climate conducive to quality and progression in composing for the 8–12 age group, and arguably well beyond. One is an approach that has expectations of each pupil as an individual to develop her or his own composing pathway. This entails at least some opportunity for pupils to work on self-devised composing projects, based on their own skills and interests. The other lies in establishing the class as a community of composers, working alongside each other and together, generating interest, curiosity and a supportive context in which individuals feel able to take the risks inherent in any creative work. Gamble (1984) sees it as part of a teacher's role to ensure that 'musical experiences in the classroom take place in an atmosphere where personal relationships are warm, sympathetic, tolerant and respectful', arguing that children are more likely 'to develop sensitivity to music while at the same time developing sensitivity to people'. It is hard to overrate the importance of this.

More specifically, aims for composing development for this age group might be:

- to encourage each child to recognise and develop their own composing pathway, building on personal musical skills, interests and imagination
- to create ongoing composing opportunities for individual and collaborative work in the context of the class and school as a musical community
- to increase the skills, understanding and vocabulary that will support composing development
- to provide a musical environment that will enrich, interest and challenge children in pursuing their own creative work
- to enable children's music to be performed, presented, saved, and listened to by different audiences across a range of contexts.

In working towards such aims, while the class will always be the basic teaching unit, composing activity may well differ considerably from one pupil to another. In planning for composing, it is worth giving this some careful thought. Curriculum requirements may be that every pupil learns composing, but this need not imply that all pupils undertake the same composing activities. This is often an assumption and may be seen as the easiest or perhaps the only practical option. Experience shows, however, that this is not the case. It is quite possible to manage composing in such a way that individual enterprises and class projects combine and interact. The resulting increase in pupils' motivation and the greater amount of work produced independently makes teaching considerably easier, since a momentum builds up which carries work along. The composing pathway taken by each child can be tracked by enabling work to be collected on tape or disc and by expecting pupils to keep composing notebooks. These can be used for recording composing activity and making self-assessments of pieces once completed. Notations can be included where appropriate and pupils can enter comments on music listened to and notes from class work. Composing notebooks, together with audio recordings, contribute evidence for teacher assessment and provide a record of progress that can go with the child into the next class. A majority of pupils can manage these effectively and simplified recording sheets can be used to help those that find it hard.

A teaching approach that balances individual and class work in this way enables many pupils to reach higher standards, since each can work to the limits of their imagination, skills and experience. The chapter that follows looks at the earlier stages of children's independent composing in relation to teaching composing in class-based settings. This leads to a consideration of how class work in turn contributes to individual development. The musical focus reflects the considerations that seem most to occupy children as composers during this phase, namely the development of new ways of structuring their music in relation to its intended outcomes or purposes.

Individual composing pathways

Before considering how children learn through composing in class settings therefore, it is worth reflecting on the music children make for themselves. The class teacher who wants to maximise composing development with this age group must reverse some thinking that has often pervaded music teaching. Instead of assuming that music lessons are the starting point in which pupils learn the skills they may later be able to apply to composing for themselves, the expectation can be that pupils bring with them composing experience on which they can build. Music in school therefore ensures that children develop their skills and understanding further, enabling them to become increasingly ambitious in their ideas for their own composing.

The teacher will need to start work with any new class by discovering what musical activity children are already involved in that includes, or has potential for, composing activity. Much of the experience younger children bring is grounded in play activity. For the middle years age group, the most significant additional experience is often related to instruments they learn, other music groups they take part in or the use they make of home computers and other music technology. 'You can get this game on the Playstation called music and you can mix all your own music and stuff' (T, aged 9). Although it might be expected that all this applies to only a small proportion of pupils, it can be surprising how many children are involved in some form of music beyond the classroom. Such backgrounds might include family instruments played informally, marching bands, brigades and cadet forces, dance and theatre groups, and children involved through their parents in folk and rock bands, samba schools, drumming or religious music. At the stage when the processes of composing are still so bound up with the need to work 'hands-on' with musical sound, these activities have a considerable influence on the music children compose and the kind of musical thought that lies within it. Performing skills readily lead into doodling, improvising and on into making music of one's own. 'I play the cornet and the piano and sometimes if my Gran comes round, I get her to listen and I play her things I haven't learnt yet. I make them up...' (B, aged 9). The styles of music children hear and play become the styles most available to them for composing. Music in class can build on and extend such experience, but it needs to include it.

It is crucial in school to make every effort to acknowledge and draw on children's very real and increasing instrumental skills in relation to their composing, and to tap into their growing understanding of how music works in the world around them. Instrumental skills can easily become overlooked when composing is seen simply as confined to a brief class activity carried out with school instruments in the music lesson. For the most motivated pupils, this can, at worst, develop into a situation where they are busy being real composers at home and then pretending to compose in school situations which take no account of the rest at all. If music opportunities in school are stimulating and challenging enough, however, and the encouragement is there, most pupils are eager to bring music made in class and beyond together and this helps to build a strong sense of musical self-esteem and identity. Some differentiation of composing pathways becomes important in allowing pupils to work to their strengths and interests. Composing evolves through a series of work in which each piece leads on to another. If this progression is to be taken seriously, it will need to be based firmly in each child's experience.

Instrumental learning and composing

Children who are already learning instruments are often to be found extending this activity into inventing music of their own, with or without adult encouragement. This may start as a form of play: improvising with sounds and ideas that come to hand, diverting from the official demands of 'practice' on an instrument. A child may just enjoy pursuing musical imagination through the voice or fingers, particularly as their skills in producing and controlling musical sound increase. The technique that has been acquired, possibly even reluctantly, is put to personal and expressive use. Learning an instrument involves learning 'pieces'. These provide a ready prompt for children to make pieces of their own, and to notate them in the musical language they are learning to read.

R, aged nearly 9, makes a recording which intersperses tunes she's learnt and her own improvisations and compositions for the instruments she is learning to play. The tape includes an introduction and linking commentary as the listener is presented with music that ranges across a variety of tempo, mood and character. The music is obviously absorbing her as a player and is dynamically and expressively very alive. At the same time she has an awareness of audience which comes to the fore between the performances. The commentary uses the kind of formulae that might be heard during a radio show or in a compered concert:

> This is gonna be called 'Oompah' . . .
> Thank you, that was my composement.
> Just got to warm up . . . that wasn't a piece. This is the proper thing now.
> Do you want me to play the 'cello now? I'm just going to set it up. I'll carry on buzzing so you'll know I'm here.

This first piece is called 'In a Garden'.
Bye for now.

The composed music arises from a mixture of improvisation, in which familiar finger patterns lead the way, and aural experimentation with what the instrument can do. Each piece is carefully brought to an end using conventional devices such as slowing up, fading out or definite chord or sustained note finishes.

> Tuning up on the recorder leads into a series of long held notes and trills. The main recorder piece uses a repeating rhythmic pattern that includes some very high sounds, breathy at first, but becoming purer.
>
> A 'cello melody played on one string is easily moved across to another resulting in a sequence, the same melodic pattern played at a different pitch. As the music takes hold, double stopping comes in and some very fast repeated note effects, accented and powerful, which again exploit the sense of what the instrument is capable of giving voice to.
>
> The piano music uses left-hand triads, major and minor, in several different pianistic formulations – block and broken chords and an 'Alberti' bass, with a right hand tune over the top.

This music is rooted in the instrumental technique available and in familiar styles, yet it is audibly creative as new ideas suggest themselves and are worked with. Making her own music takes R into instrumental capabilities well beyond those demanded by her usual repertoire. The sense of drama of the solo performance continues all the way through. In this case, the music was recorded as a collection to be saved or shared. In terms of aural understanding, musical creativity and instrumental skills, the learning potential is considerable. Yet such music is often heard, if overheard at all, as 'off task'. The child is not 'practising properly'.

Verney (1991) shows how composing can be integrated into the teaching of individual instruments with beneficial effects on motivation and instrumental progress. Verney devised a programme in which children beginning violin lessons at age 7–8 are asked to compose their own tunes right from the start. The composing continues, following each stage of acquiring a new technique, note or finger position on the instrument. He found that the resulting compositions far exceeded expectations and that children's pieces are more adventurous and set greater challenges for instrumental technique than the music usually presented. This systematic kind of approach has the advantage of establishing an expectation of pupils that they will both play and compose music for themselves, and there are also clearly beneficial consequences for instrument learning. It has the disadvantage of allowing the sequence of playing techniques to drive compositional ideas along a pathway whose logic is tied to the instrument in question rather than to more wide ranging musical ideas. Some unexpected possibilities arise from this, however. Verney gives five examples of 7 year old boys' tunes composed for open strings alone. These show 'how the children enjoy the possibilities of repetition and the contrasting sounds when notes are far apart' (Verney 1991: 250–1). Interesting compositional thought processes are present in each tune and it is clear that, as well as responding to the potential for very big leaps and bold or more contained contours, the boys have been able to play with the permutations of line shape available in structuring their melodies. There is compositional thinking here that is transferable for use with wider musical material later. Children are encouraged to listen to each other's work and ideas are extended.

Of course, the choice of instrument also helps to define the range and style of repertoire which children encounter most. Whatever this is, it is obvious that the music they play on instruments they are learning will also influence their musical imagination and aural expectations. The Hope Valley Squeeze Box Project (Burke 1996) illustrates vividly how acquiring instrumental skills flows readily into composing within the traditions belonging to the instrument one plays. Large numbers of children in a Derbyshire primary school learn to play a whole range of 'squeeze boxes', from piano accordions to various concertinas. In keeping with the traditional approach to these instruments, children learn a large number of traditional tunes aurally and 'are encouraged to use their inner voice or 'ear' to both learn and retain melodies'.

> Traditional music is based around simple structures that lend themselves very readily to composition. The instruments, particularly the melodeon, are conducive to improvisation. The melodic buttons are arranged in thirds so that one needs only to push and press each consecutive button in turn to produce a pleasing arpeggio pattern. Several children have produced good tunes through experimenting around the structure of a reel, waltz, hornpipe or jig.
>
> (Burke 1996: 12)

Whatever the instrument or musical style, it seems good sense to encourage children to bring music composed for their own instruments into school. A class composing forum (see page 89) provides the opportunity to hear some of this music, or it can be made available for individual listening by tape or disc on a listening centre or computer. The composing issues which arise are likely to be similar to those arising in other circumstances and sharing music for different instruments can become part of the class's learning programme as a whole. A useful follow-up, particularly for older pupils, is to pair up to compose for each other's instruments. This is the next stage in coming to understand the possibilities and technical requirements in composing for different instruments. Building knowledge of pitch ranges, or what is easy or harder to play on different instruments continues as children move on into secondary school. The pragmatic approach of learning from a friend by composing for them is a useful bridge.

Music groups and composing

E, just 8 and a member of the school recorder group, was busy with music at home in the weeks leading up to a school concert performance. She told the teacher about a recorder piece she was composing and seemed to be working very hard on it. Each week she would report on progress but brought the music into school only when she was satisfied it was complete. E's conception of composing is not only to make the music up, but also to write it down (see page 81). Just as R is giving her music the contextual trappings of conventional presentations, E is replicating the format she has learned within the recorder group of working with music that is notated on a page. Her score is a good example of the later stages of emergent music writing, meticulous in using a full range of flats, naturals and sharps as well as time and key signatures, rests, bar lines and dots. The pitches are all accurate, including the ambiguous B and B flat contrasts. The barlines are still rather arbitrary and the repeat opening of the second line is differently placed in the bar each time. Much later she realised and confirmed with the teacher that sharp, natural and flat signs are conventionally placed on the same line or space as the note they apply to. In such circumstances the new knowledge falls easily into place because the child already understands its application. The tune itself offers a melodic line which is shaped in a mixture of steps and wider intervals which, no doubt unconsciously, take on a kind of symmetrical balance by inversion at the outset and then develop into more extended phrases later on.

Such a piece might continue to be performed solo by the composer or it might be learnt and performed by the whole group. Whichever is the case 'My Song' remains E's property and when pieces like this are freely forthcoming from children they provide the opportunity for the teacher to incorporate children's own work into the group's repertoire. A tune like this can be a cue for the class or group together to start looking at new compositional issues. In this case these might be:

- the shaping and phrasing of melodies – the contours might be drawn in the air – feeling how the melody moves, where it jumps and where it steps
- the phrasing of melodies composed for wind instruments or voices in relation to where the performer can take a breath: the group can investigate how long a breath will last and the effect of breathing at different places, suggesting where to breathe
- the feeling in a tune of having Bs and B flats and Fs and F sharps close together: this will lead to careful listening and perhaps hearing the line with and without the flats and sharps

Investigation might be followed up by listening to other recorder music or by comparing this melody with others in repertoire. The teacher can encourage children's composing contributions and support work by listening and by

Figure 6.1 'My song'

including pieces in group rehearsals. Pieces composed for music groups might be taken to class music and included in tape or disc collections and notebook entries. Rehearsals of a school band or orchestra might include some sessions in which pupils make or practise compositions for smaller groups.

Making composing opportunities

It is not only in connection with instrumental learning that children of this age bring a strong individual motivation for composing. There are pupils who quickly make use of every opportunity offered to follow a quite independent programme of composing which appears to be self-sufficient and self-directed in every sense. These pupils are not necessarily seen as musical types since this characterisation is often reserved for those who are known to play instruments. Yet the pupils for whom composing is compelling despite a lack of experience of performing skills are likely to be the most imaginative and skilful composers of all, since the composing drive for them appears to comes from their interest in working creatively with musical sound. If time, space, opportunity and access to resources can be made available on some kind of regular basis, independent composing can be opened up to a wider group of pupils. This might be managed as a lunchtime or after school club or, if appropriate space and supervision is available, as provision which can be used at appropriate times during the day.

N's father is an amateur country and western singer and although N plays no instrument proficiently, he has a sense of performance which may well come from being at least familiar with the kind of confidence, projection, drama and use of dynamics that performing for an audience calls up. After an initial session of free improvisation exploring syncopated rhythm patterns and chord changes on a chordal dulcimer, there was no stopping N's stream of ideas for compositions which would be devised, rehearsed – alone or with others – and then kept in repertoire. Over the year between his eighth and ninth birthday, N produced a series of pieces that although not polished in performance had vividly strong and diverse dramatic character. These included:

- 'The Drums', for two players stationed at opposite sides of a room
- Piece for dulcimer with chime bars
- Piece for solo glockenspiel
- Piece for two glockenspiels face to face, based on mirror and symmetry
- 'Hey ho the merry oh', in a narrative, declamatory style, with chorus
- 'Giddy up', a piece for two voices singing in canon, with rhythm backing
- 'Staying alive', a very slow sustained melodic piece for a small keyboard, played at three different octaves in succession (see page 86)
- Dance piece for two players with assorted percussion, using a 'Spanish' rhythm pattern and swapping instruments in and out of a shifting texture
- 'The Church Bells' inspired by a return to chime bars
- Drum improvisation.

In every case, N sets out to compose with an idea he's had for a piece. These ideas seem to arise from various sources: things he's seen and heard musically, the possibilities that an instrument or another player offers, or a musical technique, such as inversion or canon that he thinks might work and sets out to explore. His sense of a musical piece as a dramatic whole is strongly in evidence all through this collection and there is a unity of conception in each that comes across despite the rudimentary performance skills at his disposal. Children like N seem to approach composing as composers from the outset. This suggests that just as we look to instrumentalists with higher expectations of performance, we might look to other children with higher expectations of composing. Composing and performing are very different arts and their relationship has many different forms.

Other pupils take very readily to composing on computers, drum machines or sequencers or by using the multi-track facility on keyboards. Here the relationship between composing and performing is bypassed in another way, in that the technology itself stands in for performing skills. This frees the child to compose and listen back, having inputed the musical ideas either in stages or in step time, avoiding the need to play the music as it is to be heard. H, age 11, made comparisons between composing on her own instrument, the flute, and on the computer (Lanyon 1998). The musical structuring of her computer music was less satisfactory to her than the 'playing around on my instrument' which she does at home. Since the computer offered rhythm as well as melody staves, H began each piece by putting in a rhythm track. This was based on a repeating rhythm, not unconnected to the discovery of the copy and paste facility. She commented that this was a good way to 'make good drum beats'. Melodically she built her work in stages, listening back, singing and tapping her feet as she worked. In the end she decided that she preferred to work from an instrument. For other pupils, the computer opens new possibilities in composing which lead to progress that would not otherwise have been possible.

When children in school are offered open opportunities to compose their own music, the insights gained from listening to the work produced are probably the most valuable indicators of what it will be most appropriate to work towards in class sessions. I have always found it most straightforward to draw the focus for teaching from features observed in children's recent work, usually the work produced independently rather than from commissioned tasks. Often this can be made explicit for the children. For instance, a new topic looking at scales and modes might be introduced by saying: 'I noticed in D's xylophone piece that she was working with a particular set of notes and that these notes gave the music a very particular sound and flavour. We're going to listen to the piece again and then go on to find out how using different note sets affects the sound of the music made' (see page 86). The chosen musical feature may or may not have been part of the composer's original intentions. Either way, this strategy has the strength of endorsing the music a child has produced and at the same time modelling an important composing process, that of constantly learning from music itself by investigating further or new possibilities. It should also help to ensure that the musical focus of teacher-led work is well matched to the current range of musical understanding and perspective across the class. The following examples show some of the common preoccupations for composers of this age group. Any of the features described could become topics to be followed up in class.

Finding musical forms

As children begin to work for themselves with the idea of constructing a piece, they find their way into the music from different expressive or organisational points of view. Just as they have very different compositional purposes (see page 28), so the ways in which their music takes shape are equally varied. There is no one way to compose. Making a tune, for example, is a quite different enterprise from composing a drumming piece designed to be loud, vigorous and exciting. As a concern for the form and structure of the music begins to come to the fore, both children and teachers need to engage in finding structures that work for the expressive or other purposes of each new piece. A crucial aspect of assessing any piece of music is to ask how far it works 'in its own terms'. That is to say, each piece has its own purposes, musical ideas, and sound world of timbres and textures. The final shape of the piece must be such as to allow these to work musically together. This has to be judged aesthetically by listening, and, in the early stages, composers must learn to trust their own listening judgements. The following discussion may help to indicate some common musical issues arising for children during the early stages of composing complete pieces of their own. Although these examples are mainly drawn from the age group they most characterise, that is from 8 up to perhaps 10 years old, the same features are frequently found in the early work of students of any age.

There are many different ways of thinking about the structural aspects of music and different vocabularies reflect these. For example:

- *structures viewed architecturally* may be described in terms of being built, perhaps in sections and subsections, or built in layers on a foundation:– a drone, a bass riff, a ground or a repeating pattern, or even shaped, perhaps melodically like arch
- *structures arising from interaction between performers* may be described as turn-taking, joining in, following on from, conversation, call and response, imitative, or as chasing or following, such as in a round or canon
- *structures experienced dramatically* may be described in terms of conflict, surprise, opposition, reconciliation, or in terms of unfolding events: inevitable, unexpected, forceful or gradually calming.

Structures may also be recognised as standard musical forms: song forms, for instance, of verse, verse and chorus, ballad or dialogue, or dance forms with particular rhythmic characteristics, such as disco or waltz. Discussing musical structures often depends on time-based concepts such as those of before, after, beginning, going on, changing, altering, gradually, suddenly, transforming, returning, repeating, lengthening shifting and so on. As children learn to construct their music into shorter or longer pieces, such vocabulary can be introduced when listening to the music and reviewing either work in progress or finished products. The way pupils describe their work also gives an insight into how they are thinking about its structures in relation to whatever it is they are aiming to do musically.

The ways in which children become able to think musically in their heads, are crucial to the creative handling of the very abstract concepts of time and temporal experience that underlie musical structures. Being able to grasp temporal relationships and to envisage how the experience of a set of musical relationships of this kind is going to impact on a listener, aesthetically or dramatically, requires a considerable degree of operational thought. It is towards this level and quality of musical thinking that children's composing has to move if it is to become more than just mechanistic orderings and sequencing of sound. Children have to learn to imagine as a whole a musical structure that can only ever be experienced as unfolding in time. They must be able to 'fast forward' or 'rewind' mentally as they work out different parts of the music. And they have to be able to hold in mind how changes to any one part of the music will impact on the effect of the whole. These skills are acquired only through considerable experience. One vital role for teachers in supporting this can be in finding analogies and ways of visualising sequences in time or experiencing time in movement, which can help pupils gain understanding of the invisible and intangible qualities of music.

Composing alone

Composed tunes form a huge category of children's early and ongoing work, particularly that made alone. These are often composed by a process of finding them out through singing or playing. It is almost as if, once a beginning has been captured, the rest has only to be revealed rather than actively put together. Exploration of melodic structures is also an exceptionally rich field for class composing investigations. This may include looking at songs that are part of the class repertoire but also exploring melodies drawn from the countless different traditional world music repertoires of dance, celebration and lament.

N's melody 'Staying alive' for keyboard (page 86; also see page 82) has a haunting shape which comes partly from the aspiring opening phrases, which move up in pitch three times in succession, and partly from the slow, repeated rhythm pattern, used all the way through until the final phrase. He has also managed, consciously or not, to build the tension through past the midpoint of the tune by two unexpected moves. The first is to repeat motif 'a' once more than anticipated. The second is to drop the lower note in this motif to make a

Figure 6.2 Middle years compositions

fall of a whole octave in its final repeat. The ending, different altogether, seems to restore equilibrium and resolve the whole tune. The melody is grounded solidly in C major. It is played three times: once at pitch, an octave higher and then an octave lower. Here the structuring seems to come from the dramatic intention of establishing mood, but is nevertheless very architectural in outcome.

D's melody (page 86) is architectural through and through and is composed simply as a melody to be enjoyed. Confidently played on a xylophone, whose notes have been rearranged to suit her purposes, she later called in H to shadow the rhythm of the tune on a pair of claves. The piece has a fast tempo and comes across as very assured, using the technique of repeating the main four bar section (A) three times with different tune sections (B and C) in between. The main tune is in itself symmetrical, with a rising phrase and a falling one, and so is section C. A more definite ending is used to modify A on its final hearing. Based on a very distinctive note set, a scale from D to D . With B flats throughout, this piece could make an ideal springboard into follow-up class work on the scales and modes that can be used for tune-making. Pupils can experiment with well-known scales or assemble their own note sets and improvise or compose melodies restricted to them. Alternatively, the structure of the melody could be used as a starting point for investigating tunes that are built in sections.

Of course, not all children's melodic structures are so 'four square'. S's short melody (page 86) is an example of a piece that is carefully structured but sounds less conclusive, four 'unsquare' in fact. In her terms it is very complete and the rationale for it is clear. However, the resulting change of metre midway has an additional impact that she hasn't accounted for. Sometimes irregularity works imaginatively and well; here the structure seems to be at odds with the outcome. A's melody develops an opening motif that is repeated and then reversed quite conventionally. He then comes under the spell of the alternation it contains of the notes A and A sharp, very close together, and weaves a more improvisational ending out of these, moving them up an octave and speeding up while fading out. He later described this as a 'crying tune' and it certainly draws its structuring from both architectural and dramatic musical thinking. Both of these would lead well into looking at asymmetrical melodies and A's piece suggests one of many ways in which an idea can develop gradually as the melody goes on.

Composing together

Children working in partnership are able to explore structures that are based more perhaps on the interactions themselves than on an abstract or mathematical type of approach. This is valuable in opening up a different set of ways of structuring music, offering equally rich opportunities for exploration. At the most basic level, this can be the sheer enjoyment of playing and starting and stopping together. A group piece played by four 8 year olds, two on tambours and two on tambourines exploits exactly this power. They play together in twos, alternating fast beating with fast shaking. There are silences between each turn and their eye contact is intent as they judge the moment to start and to stop together. The resulting music is a dramatic structure of sound and silence, with the two contrasting blocks of different timbre. Its conception, though, is as partnership and turn-taking. It lends itself to an analogy of sound and silence with movement and stillness and would give a way into music that is not beat based, but ordered in more rhythmically free ways. N, in partnership with L, composed a piece aptly called The Drums (see page 82). This involves two players of large drums in an interactive drama played out from opposite sides of the room, with one player mostly echoing the other. The spatial dimension gives the music an impressive effect and also impacts on the lengths of time allowed between episodes. The musical structure in this piece depends on rhythm patterning but also on dynamic alternations, which are suggested by the basis of the piece being the relationship between two players.

More conventionally, 'The Drummer Boy', composed by A and S (aged 9), takes the following structure:

> Recorder introduction, using the notes B, A and G.
> Sung verse, in which the phrase 'I am the drummer boy' alternates with the recorder and a military drum pattern played together.
> Sung line, 'I am the drummer boy', followed by a military drum pattern.
> Drum coda, using alternate beats on the head and the rim of the drum.

The musical ideas and the text came about in response to the experience of hearing the recorder and the snare drum together. The timbres evoke a musical style that is taken up. The piece is then structured as a miniature dramatisation, drawing on the different combinations available from the two players. Working together also leads into melodic and harmonic musical interactions. C and S, also aged 9, composed a piece in which they set out to make

Figure 6.3 Composing together

variations also based on combinations of two players. In this case, their initial tune was played first in unison, with a harmonic ending, then in a rhythmic variation and finally in a round (above). This is a mixture of structuring arising from both interactive and architectural approaches. It introduces the idea of generating music by exploring sameness and difference as well as polyphonic textures.

In the case of A and T (10 years old), the combination of two players led into their first venture into harmony (above). Though this was at the simplest of levels, the discovery came as a revelation to the players and is an example of a frequent occurrence for children (often younger than this): reaching the point at which harmony becomes of interest. Here one player maintains a single two-note chord while the other builds a melody over the top. This tiny piece was made at the end of a session involving extensive improvisation and experimentation. As is often the case, a major step forward results in an outcome which seems almost a step back. This piece is a cue to introduce ways of building chords from intervals of a third and to look at simple harmonic accompaniments to known or newly composed tunes. Conversely, classwork on this topic will lead into the idea being taken up in pupils' music.

Once pupils realise that the music they make will be taken seriously, in the sense of listened to and accepted, composing starts to build its own momentum in the classroom. Whether pupils' own work is done outside or inside school, the effect of its being heard and acknowledged accumulates. Children borrow ideas from each other and gain confidence in their own capacities to try out new possibilities. If, in addition, class work makes some connection with music brought by individuals, this in turn reinforces the sense of high expectations and of moving forward. This creates a more positive basis than leaving composing activities as a series of 'one-offs', or worse still focusing all discussion on 'how could it have been better?' While children are usually all too conscious of how it could have been better, they are often less aware of the techniques they *have* used or of the impact of their work on other listeners. A good principle in teaching composing is to work more with what is there than with what isn't. Finally, individual children can be encouraged to think of their work as an ongoing series. As each piece is finished they can consider what direction they want to take next. It is in providing the kind of rich musical environment that stimulates ideas for new pieces that work with the class as a whole comes into its own.

Composing and class music

If composing in school is to be based on an approach which balances individual composing pathways with work carried out in class, approaches to composing in class situations have to be structured accordingly. The shared learning which takes place through the programme of class activities finds its way into the work of individual pupils. Some composing activities take place in school, either in lesson time or at other times when the opportunity can be made available. Other composing takes place out of school, as homework or as voluntary activity. If children's composing is to reach the levels of which they are capable, class music sessions will need to make room for and acknowledge work of all these kinds and to set high expectations of children's work. The following quite distinct kinds of class music sessions can each contribute to pupils' composing development in different ways.

Composing forum

Using the class music lesson as a composing forum is a way of linking work done by individuals or groups into the main music agenda for the class. It enables pupils to learn from each other and helps develop all pupils' understanding of composing. The format is that of a listening and discussion group, to which contributions are brought by members of the class. Contributions may be:

- performances of finished compositions, live or recorded on tape or disc
- compositions in progress
- reports of composing ideas, work in progress, suggestions, discoveries or problems
- self-assessment summaries or composition notebook entries.

The forum provides the opportunity to listen and discuss completed compositions that may have been made in school or beyond, self-initiated or as homework. Music can be brought, performed and listened to with time for enjoyment and reflection. Discussion may be minimal or may focus on particular aspects: describing the musical structures themselves, discussing how different class members respond to the music, or investigating the processes through which it was put together. The teacher might use this opportunity to highlight new musical ideas or vocabulary in relation to the music offered, or to make connections with other composers' work that can be listened to alongside.

Hearing music in progress encourages children to become aware of different ways of working towards the musical result that they want. Discussion might cover alternative scenarios for what happens next in a piece, how several fragments might be joined together, or whether there are too many or too few ideas. Asking children to talk about compositions they are currently doing or planning for, or to air aspects of composing they find difficult, can stimulate others to think more widely about their own work. Troubleshooting and problem-solving can become co-operative ventures. This not only gives support to individuals but models for the whole class some different ways of working. It is helpful if discussion is referred back to musical sound wherever possible, with demonstration and listening, so that the principle of trusting listening judgement above all else is promoted. On completion of a class project, a forum might be used for pupils to bring self-assessments or notes they've made keeping track of their work. Here too it is helpful for children to hear other people's thoughts and relate these to their own reflections. Reinforcing the idea that each piece of composing teaches you something which can be brought forward into later work helps to maintain a sense of personal progression for each child.

Kirwan (1997) used a class debate approach as part of a song-writing project with a mixed 7–11 year old class. After each child had produced a song of their own, made at home and brought into school, she introduced a questionnaire to initiate reflection on attitudes to song writing, knowledge about song features, perceived difficulties in composing songs and evaluation of their own work. This laid the groundwork for class debate about song features, based on the songs composed by the children. From this discussion the class generated their own framework to use for future song analysis. The value of co-operative work which supports individual composing is that children learn together and from each other while applying their learning to their own music.

In addition to what pupils bring, the composing forum can include visiting composers talking about their work. Professional composers, composers writing in local bands, choirs or theatre groups, parents, friends, older pupils in the school, can all help to widen children's perceptions of what it is to compose and give insight into creative ideas and working methods. Video extracts introducing composers' work in any musical style or genre can also broaden the children's perspectives.

A composing forum works best when the session is focused enough to give some depth, lively and stimulating, and not too long. Clearly it is not possible for everyone to be heard every time. These occasions are best as regular events, with the 'agenda' prepared for, and a rolling programme of pupils taking turns to be in the spotlight. Just as composition work improves if fewer projects are undertaken but with more time and quality given to each, so a forum might aim to include everyone's work once a term as a minimum, more often if possible. Each child can be expected to take an active part on each occasion, however, and the skills of listening, noticing, questioning and debating can be worked on as explicit learning points for the whole class. The teaching skill is to ensure that each event is interesting, challenging, and thought provoking.

Improvisation workshop

If children are to continue to expand their aural ideas and understanding, workshops in which improvisation is the main activity are an important part of the programme. Improvisation can be managed as a class activity in several ways:

* the whole class singing or playing together

- the class in a circle with a small group of performers in the middle; these improvise from their own ideas while others listen and give feedback afterwards
- members of the class suggest a 'rule' or a set of ideas on which to base the improvisation and a pair or group of performers try these out; all listen and review the music in relation to the initial idea.

Recording improvisation so that it can be watched and listened to again after the event can lead to a greater awareness of the musical result. Pupils can be encouraged to extend class work by improvising in pairs or groups outside lesson time. Learning outcomes in relation to composing might be:

- exploring musical sounds and structures creatively, discovering how they behave
- learning to listen and respond aurally and intuitively
- building confidence in thinking in sound, inventing 'on the wing' and taking musical risks
- learning to interact with others musically, finding new musical structures based on interaction.

Improvisations can be completely free or can start with a 'rule' of some kind. Free improvisation has the advantage that it enables participants to respond to what they hear in an immediate way, perhaps thinking less and listening more. If pupils are confident enough to just launch into the music, this allows intuitive responses to determine the music. Depending on experience, it also enables maximum interaction to take place. Some pupils, however, find it hard enough to think about their own music without taking on board what others are doing. Introducing one or more rules into the improvising context offers a great deal of scope for pupils to explore particular creative ideas, and to test these almost as hypotheses. Children quickly become interested in devising rules of different kinds and predicting how these will affect the musical outcome. A rule might govern:

- who plays or sings, when and how much: this will affect texture and structure
- what timbres or kinds of sounds are available: short sounds only, for example or humming and unvoiced sounds together
- the note set, scale or mode to be used or a drone or bass riff or ground
- a melodic or rhythmic idea which is to be explored and played with
- the overall shape of the music: for example, it must build slowly and then reverse back to the starting point
- a musical or interactive process: for example, join in one at a time, copying someone and altering it somehow; base everything you do on shapes of five or three

- the time frame of the music: the piece will last one minute, everyone will play once and then stop
- the mood or dramatic quality to be set.

Improvisation is a skill in itself and not to be underrated but it can also lead to ideas for composing. Hearing improvised music and discussing responses to what happened can contribute to pupils' understanding of how musical structuring leads to certain aesthetic effects. Improvisation is a good way to stimulate children's interest in this, particularly as the quality of unpredictability lends additional dramatic value. And if a new musical idea is being introduced to the class, improvising may be a more effective way to explore it than through a composing task.

Composing projects

Given a climate in which children's individual composition work is flourishing, supported by the forum and workshop strategies above, the composition projects which are usually the mainstay of planning for composition begin to have a more specific role. This is to focus work on a particular musical topic, one that is chosen to match pupils' abilities, understanding and their current composing needs. Some topics arise directly from the work of a group of pupils. Others may be chosen because of a more general readiness for the next stage developmentally, for example, moving into work with simple chords or needing to enrich ideas about melodic shapes and structures. A class music topic might be linked to music of a particular genre, style, time or place. Alternatively it might be linked to language, drama, dance or art work, such as a song-writing project, music for a production or a cross-curricular investigation. Composing projects may be a small part of a unit. More effectively, they can be staged over several weeks, involving in-depth explorations of composing techniques, and several stages of composing and performance all set in the context of listening to the work of other composers.

Within such topics, setting a specific class composing task and asking pupils to work on it alone or in groups becomes a means of:

- extending pupils' skills in using a technique or feature as composers
- gaining a better understanding of a musical aspect or feature
- enriching musical imagination and experience by discovering new possibilities
- challenging pupils to respond creatively to a given commission and within a set time.

The teacher also gains insight into how each pupil or group of pupils is understanding the task in question.

Class projects often suffer from too little time, poor working conditions leading to noise, and the pressure on resources which results from all working at once. Trying to set, carry out, record and review a composition within a single session, even a longish session, is a recipe for low-level work in any children's terms. As an exercise in introducing an idea, it may be justifiable, but this distinction will need to be made for pupils so that a higher expectation of composition can be maintained. Of course, some people work well creatively when under pressure of time and it is quite possible for excellent compositions to be made very fast indeed, particularly when pupils have their own purposes and starting points clear at the outset. The difficulty arises when class composing projects are the sole format offered, since these possible advantages do not work for everyone. If the difficulty of negotiating work in a group is an added factor, ensuring a quality composing experience for every pupil is extremely hard. If there is room for flexibility, additional times to practise in between sessions, work spread over two or more sessions, or a really substantial time slot found as an occasional provision all enhance work done in these ways.

During the primary and middle years, enormous progress is made in composing. Perhaps one of the chief developments from the teacher's point of view is the possibility that becomes available for a genuinely two-way link between individual work and the introduction and investigation of new ideas in class. Alongside this, children are ready to reflect on their work with increasing awareness, and their performing and composing skills increase considerably. Working effectively in groups becomes a real possibility, discussed further in the next chapter. Above all, these years are characterised by a musical confidence, energy and enthusiasm that is fuelled through the satisfaction children find in their music beginning to sound more like the music they encounter beyond school. This period of confidence is often temporary. As children move into adolescence, musical self-awareness brings its own setbacks.

Chapter 7

Musical style
Children aged 10–14

If learning to handle music as a time-based medium is one of the long haul aspects of compositional development in the middle years, another is the ongoing struggle to make your music sound the way you imagine it. Part of this is the relatively straightforward, though tough, problem of knowing what it is you are hearing in your mind; which pitches, which harmony, which instrumental combinations. If the aural images are reasonably clear and strong, the skills that address these difficulties are as much those of aural analysis and basic theoretical knowledge as anything, though these skills are hard won and take much practice to acquire. More fundamentally however, when pupils say that their music 'doesn't sound right', 'doesn't sound like I'm thinking it' or 'isn't the way I want it', the underlying issue is often one relating to musical style. In many guises, it is questions of style in music that form the main agenda for the period of development during which young composers move into adolescence, although these questions begin to surface much earlier. And style is not just a matter of what you do; it is also and essentially about the way you do it.

As children become increasingly able to listen critically to their own music and make composing judgements based on standing back as audience and thinking about how to adjust work in progress, they refer what they hear more and more to their perceptions of 'real' music. With developing self-awareness comes the potential for losing confidence, since awareness directed at oneself is also available for making comparisons with others. A major role for teachers, as pupils begin this difficult transition, is to help children maintain faith in themselves as learners. As apprentice composers, children need time, room and acceptance to continue making their music, with better and worse results, while they painstakingly acquire the relevant skills and find a sense of identity. There is no point in teachers trying to bolster confidence by denying the issue, or by constantly over-praising pupils. If there is going to be no acknowledgement of the desire to make their music sound different, and no teaching support which will help them progress in the directions they want to go, then disillusionment sets in and interest is lost. Reassurance is needed that it is trusting one's ear that is the touchstone for any composer, and that progress only comes through continuing to make and learn across a series of work. Paul McCartney described in a BBC interview how he and John Lennon first wrote songs:

> We'd go home and literally just go 'let's try and write a song'. And we wrote a few quite bad ones at first but then we started to get a little bit better, and the inspiration just came.
>
> (*Parkinson*, 3 December 1999)

An approach that recognises the difficulties can be completely positive if it is based on sustaining the spirit of quest and intense investigation that characterised children's early learning for themselves. But by this stage, the motivation is to be found from exactly the same 'real' music that lies at the root of pupils' dissatisfaction with what they produce. Just as the dissatisfaction is related to their already acquired experience of music around them, so this experience can be capitalised on. Pupils are increasingly ready and able by this stage to find out more about why the music they are modelling their own on sounds as it does, and to be more analytical about how it is made up. Sitting on the bed at home, listening repeatedly to a track and trying to play the bass line or even its rhythm on guitar is one way of starting to take music to bits in order to understand how it's made. Learning in school through style-related projects is another. Either way, the essence is in aiming for the closest possible contact with reality and the music out there, whatever it is.

Composing in school falls apart completely if it is not well linked into music in the world beyond. This is not least because from the youngest ages children have an extremely acute sense of the music they hear around them. By the middle years and as pupils transfer into secondary schooling, their aural experience of music across the range of styles offered by the culture around them is extensively ingrained in their musical perceptions. A secondary music teacher, commenting on the work of first year pupils, makes the assertion that pupils are being asked to compose with almost no experience of any models. This is quite astonishing if taken at face value and is almost equivalent to discounting all language use acquired prior to entering the school. Yet it is not uncommon to find older pupils in music classes being taught as if this were the case. Translating aural experience into the practical knowledge which is applied in the process of making one's own music is a long, ongoing pathway of skill progression. This, however, is not to be confused with the experience of musical models acquired through enculturation – just living – and in earlier years of practical music-making, formally and informally, in school and beyond. It is this experience which pupils begin to call on ever more consciously in relation to their own composing. And this is how they move themselves into the world of adult music.

Teachers have the task of uncovering the range of musical styles and models that each child brings with them. Alongside a strong peer culture of popular music of many kinds, individual pupils each have their own biography of musical influences and encounters linked to home, social, religious and ethnic backgrounds and to whatever activities they do in and beyond school. It is as much a mistake to assume that all pupils have in the way of musical background is pop music as it is to imagine that they lack experience altogether. And any broad category such as 'pop' or 'classical' or 'church' or 'folk' music needs breaking down into much more specific musical styles and genres. Where pupils do need models is in encountering how different composers handle work in progress, in many different ways.

Musical style

The growing importance of style in children's composing activities appears to emerge concurrently with the development of their wider awareness of musical style as listeners. In one sense this is completely unsurprising; it would be impossible for the former to come first. But it does seem to underline the extent to which children's powers of listening drive work in composition and the strong motivation they have as composers to move towards joining already established communities of musical usage. The implication of this for teachers is to recognise that, to a considerable extent, this aspect of music learning is active and self-driven if given the scope to be so.

Gardner (1973a), with Bridgeman, investigated sensitivity to musical styles with subjects across an age range from 6–19. He found that children listening to pairs of musical examples were able to identify when the two came from the same composition with increasing accuracy from ages 6–8 and through to 11. Beyond there, however, 14 year olds and 19 year old college students showed no marked increase in stylistic sensitivity although they displayed considerable differences in the ways they explained and justified their judgements.

> The pre-adolescents were immersing themselves in the musical selections, noting their affective and kinaesthetic effects, making free associations to previous experiences, and were then basing their judgements on whether the two parts 'felt' or 'seemed' the same. They were proceeding from the musical event to a final decision. In contrast, the adolescent subjects appeared to approach the task from the perspective of their musical knowledge. They had some familiarity with musical history and terminology, and they looked for examples of prior categories in the music they heard.
>
> (Gardner 1973a)

These differences of approach might be taken as indicative of the readiness of pupils moving into adolescence to be able to address the style question in a new, more analytical way, as well as to investigate it through really close contact with the music of other composers as models. Gardner characterises the move as being towards a more 'abstract attitude' and sees it as the emergence of 'a new kind of 'distanced' relationship to aesthetic works'. In relation to composing, this distancing might be seen as a two-way process in which it becomes possible to hear both one's own and other people's music from a more stylistically objective standpoint, hence the growing ability to make comparisons. This undoubtedly puts a new perspective on the ways in which teachers present music by other composers, of whatever style, to their pupils. Music can be investigated from the composer's point of view and with reference to what composers say about what they do. The composer John Adams, for example, when interviewed about how he sets about writing a large-scale piece, explains that he doesn't necessarily have a vision of the whole thing:

> The material you start working on is like the 'gene-pool' for the piece, and it takes time to get to know what the genetic structure, the personality of the piece is. It's like a human foetus. I can't impose an arbitrary, imagined shape or personality onto material that I really don't know myself very well. I think that's a very Germanic point of view – this business of the composer controlling the whole image. . . . I think there is a passive aspect to composing as well as an aggressive one. The passive one is very interesting. What I mean by passive is that I play the music back, I listen to it a lot and I sort of 'go with it'.
>
> (Smith and Walker Smith 1994: 8)

A statement like this makes an excellent starting point for discussion with pupils, leading perhaps to some work on the kind of listening and 'going with it' described here.

Castell (1982) carried out a study similar to Gardner's, but included examples of popular music and found a greater incidence of correct judgements with these than with classical examples, suggesting that the more immediate and intense the exposure to a particular area of music is, the more finely discriminations can be made. Popular music, however, immerses audiences in 'style' aspects that go beyond the music itself and tie musical characteristics into a whole lifestyle, including not just appearance and dress but attitudes and outlook. Pupils are likely to live style in relation to popular music in ways that go beyond their experiences of classical music, though not necessarily beyond experiences of other musical styles bound up with home family life.

Taking the wider view, Addessi et al. (1995) make the point that 'perception of style is not simply to recognise structures, the traits of a musical object, but it is a more important operation: perceiving is interpreting style'. Their study, along similar lines to those of Gardner and Castell focuses again on children's stylistic competence in relation to classical music, though with the added dimension of looking at familiarity with repertoire. For them, interpretation involves 'giving sense' and is a creative act in itself. The values involved in the musical features 'play an important role in the identification and production of style'. Seeing style as a 'consistent system of choices' is useful in relation to children's ongoing attempts to align their music with existing style systems, or ultimately to move on to adding adaptations or new style features of their own. Teachers can have a key role in introducing the knowledge pupils need of how these choices work out in musical terms at the level of rhythmic, melodic, and harmonic devices. Awareness of style, then, both gives pupils a sense of the musical worlds to which they wish their composing to relate, and is also the basis for gaining the technique to do it. This development arises as part of what Sloboda (1985) terms 'musical enculturation', as opposed to the musical training and skill development that build on such learning.

Of course, children's music has been stylistically influenced from the earliest ages. From the first, they borrow or imitate and then gradually assimilate aspects of what they hear around them. These influences are audible in both what children do and how they do it. S's drumming on bongos (Chapter 3) was heavily influenced by the tabla style he had heard in the temple and elsewhere. It arose from the imitation of how the playing was done, as much as from how it sounded. N's vocals in 'Hey ho the merry oh' (Chapter 6) were country and western in style, resulting in a rather strange fusion with the borrowing of other elements, and particularly the text, from a much more English folk style. A lengthy ballad composed by a group of 9 year old girls takes many stylistic elements in the use of lead and backing vocals from the kind of pop songs to which its creators were accustomed. F, aged 9, composes a piano piece which follows the conventions of the 18th century keyboard music she's been learning, complete with broken chord figurations, a melody passed from right hand to left hand, and melodic shapes typical of the period. The notation incorporates all the editorial phrasing, staccato and dynamic markings that she is used to seeing on the page. B, 11 years old, ambitiously composes a 'Service in C major' for full choir and organ, entirely within the genre of the Anglican music he sings daily as a choirboy in a cathedral choir.

As long as children are absorbing these features holistically, in the pre-analytical way described above, they emerge in compositions almost as colouring and flavouring, with other considerations more dominant in relation to the decisions regarding musical structure and conception. Gradually however, creating music begins to be aimed towards a particular stylistic outcome and this demands the technical ability to realise it. Young composers come to terms with this in different ways, it seems. For those composing for themselves as singers or instrumental performers who already have a fair degree of instrumental skill, it is often the case that the performing techniques they acquire through performing other people's music offer an appropriate 'vocabulary' for their own music to go alongside in a similar vein. The techniques are under the fingers, as it were, and can be used to give the raw material for composition. At the other end of the spectrum, particularly with popular music styles, there are computer composing packages which offer stylistically-based ingredients which can be assembled in a more or less failsafe way. These are not to be under-rated, even if they seem to limit possibilities, since they offer a stylistic deconstruction that is in itself a powerful learning tool. Although building the music is done through a process not unlike a construction kit, choices have to be aurally determined at every stage and the point of reference has to be a knowledge of the musical style in question. Pupils can move on to create their own musical components once they understand the elements required. Between these two approaches are pupils who work with a mixture of trial and error through performance, recording, and listening, often using technology to mediate the process at different stages.

Swanwick and Tillman found that around the age of 10 or 11 some pupils move into a 'speculative' stage (the term is attributed to Bunting 1977), during which they begin to introduce features that depart from the accepted conventions that they have begun to grasp in the period leading up to this:

> Any musical speculation clearly depends on a grasp of the vernacular, for speculation implies that there is not only sufficient manipulative ability but also a history of personal and public expressiveness; there has to be a context of socially shared musical possibilities in order to create surprises and deviations from these norms.
>
> (Swanwick and Tillman 1986: 324)

Bunting sees the 'vernacular', by which is meant 'familiar, everyday music', and 'speculative' as two modes of musical perception among others, which co-exist in children's work, coming into play or into stronger focus at different stages developmentally. He suggests:

> In the first year of secondary school we can still see all the different modes in action, but as the second year goes on there seems to be a narrowing of focus, and many children settle on our mode D (Vernacular) in preference to the others. At this age, the vernacular becomes a touchstone by which everything the child hears is measured. This may lead him to reject many types of music which at a younger age he would have welcomed. He may even reject music of his own invention . . . if it does not make sense in the vernacular he understands. Hence the familiar situation in which the teacher is impressed with a child's work, but the child himself is not.
>
> (Bunting 1977: 7)

Here, then, is the middle years equivalent of the issues facing teachers listening to much younger children's work, where an adaptation is needed if the teacher is to hear the music from a perspective informed by the pupil's perceptions and values. For many young composers at this stage, securing stylistic acceptability on the vernacular base is of real importance in giving their music credibility in their own self-assessment. From here on, Bunting suggests that the interest in the vernacular remains, though with a re-emergence (as seen earlier) of speculative thinking 'which will co-exist with the vernacular' (ibid.: 12). Somehow the teacher has to both accept this convergence and support departures from it. In this task, the musical environment offered in school can stimulate work of both kinds, but only if it relates genuinely to the widest canvas of the music heard beyond.

Real music

One of the teacher's key roles at any stage of children's composing development is to enable music made in school to remain real in its own terms while also being strongly rooted in the real music which is made and heard in the world outside. Unfortunately it is all too easy for music in the classroom to become almost an alternative musical world, so that 'school music' takes on a style of its own, not quite relating to any other music and in that sense 'unreal'. This is a problem for pupils because it cuts them off from being able to draw on their own musical experience, and thereby lowers the levels at which they can work.

Strategies that can act as an antidote to this in working with pupils at any stage might include:

- Providing as much and as varied live music in school as can be found by drawing in other members of staff, parents and carers, friends, local community groups, visitors and professional artists to improvise, perform or dance with music of all kinds of styles, to bring music they've created, composed, recorded, and to talk with, make music with and teach pupils, across formal and informal settings.
- Fostering an open door approach to music in the school generally as inclusive of the whole school community – every adult and child whatever their roles – so that music never becomes the sole province of a particular teacher, room or department.
- Maintaining and regularly refreshing the collection of recorded music used for listening in class or assembly contexts; comparing the range and proportion of styles and genres represented with those found in live music venues, major music stores, across the spectrum of radio stations, TV and Internet music programmes and sites; ensuring that selectivity is on a basis of informed awareness and breadth of outlook.
- Provision of a range of instruments, both for use in the classroom and to be learnt in individual or group lessons, that represent musical breadth, for example penny whistles as well as recorders, different drums, world percussion and other instruments, keyboards and accordion as well as piano, guitars of different sorts, and singing groups or voice lessons covering different styles.
- Provision of a wide range of music technology, for use in classroom and extra curricular work, enabling pupils to access the sound world which relates to music across a number of contemporary styles (such as popular, film, 'classical'); keyboards with memory and multitracking facilities, sequencers, computers with keyboard input and recording and editing and composing software, drum machines, recording and mixing hardware and software.
- Ensuring that musical activities represent a variety of musical styles and genres, across time, place and culture, including extra-curricular groups (such as early music, samba, traditional, folk, popular, jazz ensembles).
- Linking music listened to with the instruments available for pupils to play;

if the focus in class is on playing percussion then listening must reflect and support this, so that children hear how the instruments can sound and how they sound within different musical styles; if recorders are a main feature in a school, then hearing, for example, renaissance recorder consorts and contemporary recorder compositions must go alongside.

- Ensuring that, particularly with the older age-groups, pupils compose for the full range of vocal and instrumental performing groups and individuals available and conversely that all performers include their own or other pupil's compositions in their performing repertoire.

One school may not achieve all this and much depends on age-range and situation. However, the same principles underlie provision at whatever stage and within whatever budget, and need to be followed through as far as is possible. If the sound of music in school bears no relation to music beyond, children's composition becomes disconnected from their inner musical sense or fades away completely.

The availability of music technology is best planned for alongside rather than instead of a rich provision of acoustic instruments, and provision for this made from the youngest age-groups on. It is a double mistake if technology appears late on and instead of other instruments. Many pupils need opportunities to use both as an ongoing feature and skills progression is disrupted if there is a major switch of emphasis on transferring to a new class or school. Financial constraints are always there, but it is important to at least plan for balance and continuity in these respects, since they have such a major influence on what pupils produce.

Harmonic music

Alongside the gradually increasing importance of style for composers in these middle years, comes the move into working harmonically in the many and different ways particular musical styles demand. Again, teacher input is vital, and pupils need some carefully sequenced introductory work, best offered in short units spread over the later primary and early secondary age-phases. This, too, is an area where work with children needs to be closely related to specific musical 'languages' and genres if it is to make aural sense, and if techniques learnt are to become applicable in children's own compositions. From the teaching point of view, it is useful to offer different harmonic aspects, linked to examples of world music in which they are fundamentally at home. This is best done in conjunction with music that is available for live listening, in which the different roles of performers in contributing to the harmonic dimensions can be both seen and heard. Drones might be introduced through work on European traditional dance music or North Indian classical improvisation; moving parallel parts may be heard in early Christian and Orthodox church music traditions or in traditional vocal music; triadic choral music can be investigated in conjunction with music based in particular African traditions; three-chord tonal harmony can be researched through song accompaniment from any number of traditional or contemporary styles; instrumental bass lines can be traced through different (not just blues) popular styles; and so on.

Alongside this, pupils need time to work with chordal shapes, triads, added notes and bass lines in their own improvisatory way in order to internalise the sound and feel of the chord shift. This piano duet by two 13 year old girls (page 104) was devised and then played most mornings before school for a term, while they worked out and absorbed the effect of the chord changes they had designed. The whole focus was on the way the chords worked with the melody; other ways of spreading out the left hand chords or adding bass were not of interest. It seems as though, in the early stages, the visual consistency of the close position chords being moved while keeping the root always at the bottom contributes to the satisfaction of being able to grasp both the sound and the idea. These co-composers had stretched a point to allow for the sharpened third which contributes a major moment in this piece, and had enjoyed, rather than been disconcerted by, the way the music never returns to where it began. These were beginner composers in school and the value of staying with work in this way is significant at every stage in which pupils are trying to move forward into understanding a new aspect of the music they are working with. A single encounter in a music class resulting in a piece that is played once and never revisited cannot compare in learning terms.

As with perceptions of musical style, children's acquisition of a sense of tonality and the skills of harmonic perception seems to be a matter of enculturation and maturation, rather than of training. In this sense again, there are parallels with learning to speak a language. In the cases of musical tonality and harmony, the music to which children are most exposed is highly significant in relation to the awareness they acquire. In particular there are global divides, most strikingly east–west, between music that is essentially monodic, based on intricacy of melody within many different note-sets and 'tonalities', and music that is essentially harmonic, either in the sense of using a polyphonic, harmonic, tonally based language or in extending the use of tonality as the basis of formal structures as well (400 years or so of western classical music). For the purposes of composing, it is important that pupils are able to work with their first musical 'language', whatever that is, as well as moving between styles based on different tonal and harmonic languages in the way to which many of us have become accustomed, whatever part of the world we live in.

Moog suggests that it is not until around 7 years of age that children's awareness of the harmonic aspects of music really begins to come into play. He claims that 'the child is deaf to harmony at least up to the end of his sixth year, and probably for a long time after that' (Moog 1976: 136). This is based on observations of his subjects below this age showing no displeasure at 'cacophonies', treating them rather as 'a sort of general sound'. This seems to be a kind of extension of the phase of treating melody more as timbre than as the dominant structure in itself. The deafness is not to the sounds but to their

Figure 7.1 Piano duet

structural significance within the musical context. Hargreaves reviews research carried out on children's acquisition of harmonic skills. What emerges here is that in the areas both of perception of polyphonic melody and making distinctions between consonance and dissonance, children show through all studies a steady increase in their abilities through the primary age range and also an increase in preference for harmonisations based on consonance (Hargreaves

1986: 92–4). The research studies drawn on here are all based within a western musical context. For pupils working in such contexts, this seems to reinforce a further dimension of the self-generated imperative of young composers that their music should sound 'alright'. 'Alright' during early adolescence is likely to mean harmonically well behaved and pupils are likely to need the knowledge and skills through which to achieve 'alright' music.

Composing processes

Throughout children's composing development, musical outcomes are intrinsically bound up with the processes through which they were arrived at. In turn, these processes relate to a range of factors – thinking and working processes in themselves – but also the interaction with the instruments and other technologies through which music is produced, the individual or group settings in which it is made, and the pupils' prior musical experience. To do justice to the detail of pupils' compositional processes, particularly as they move towards producing more extended musical work, requires more space than is available in this book, although there are some examples discussed on the accompanying website. Some caution is also required in generalising from particular examples, as there are so many different facets influencing the compositional process. One more recently available avenue for investigation, that of using computers to track composing processes in music created in this medium, offers interesting possibilities. A particularly useful study, albeit with subjects slightly beyond the age-range of this book, is that carried out by Folkestad *et al.* (Folkestad 1998; Folkestad *et al.* 1998). This work is interesting, tracking the work of students with no experience of composing in an 'out-of-school activity' for which the task was to 'Use this equipment for music-making in any way you like' and with teaching interventions only to introduce and support use of the equipment and sequencer program. The findings illuminate the different approaches used and the way they revealed something of the 'dialogue' between the composers and their music. For present purposes, however, the following sections look at two wider aspects of the composing process that are very different, but both strategic in relation to musical style and the work of pupils in the later middle years.

Group composition

Each musical style brings with it differences, not just of musical language but also of vocabulary, ways of talking and learning about music and – of particular concern in relation to composing – of working processes. From the teaching point of view, one of the most strategic process differences in composing is whether pupils are to work individually or in groups. Pedagogically, there is the question of how either group or individual composing contributes to children's learning. Do pupils learn to compose better when alone or in a group? Or do they learn differently? Do some people find it easier to work creatively alone or in a group?

For younger pupils, the need for working individually at least part of the time is governed by the developmental factors of what they are able to take on board musically and how they can operate in a group socially. From the age of 9 or thereabouts, this dilemma becomes increasingly more related to musical and composing issues themselves, as they might apply to anyone learning to compose. Pragmatically, the teacher's dilemma is that of how to organise teaching with large classes of children in the limited time slot of the weekly music lesson.

In addition to these learning issues, however, teachers can also consider individual or group composing processes in relation to the 'real music' issues discussed earlier. The question arises of what range of models there are for these strategies in relation to different musical styles, and how they affect decisions about classroom work. Looking ahead, for some pupils this is also connected to vocational routes into music which involve composing, or to the interface with amateur music-making which is becoming important to them in their lives. For the middle and early secondary age group, it is as important to keep some continuity with music beyond school as it is for younger children.

Chapter 6 looked in some detail at individual composing and the ways in which it relates to the development of instrumental skills. It clearly enables pupils to work to their musical strengths and to pursue their own creative ideas. It also enables pupils to make their way through the processes of exploration, drafting and later refining work at their own speed. It allows for re-tracing steps, working out problems and memorising work, without the constraints of negotiating each stage with others. While children are still insecure in their understanding of musical structures and are building a fund of aural experience of voices and instruments, progress seems to be quicker and learning more secure if there are plenty of opportunities for working alone. Above all, perhaps, it is important for the development of children's imaginative ideas and sense of musical empowerment that it is based soundly on devising and realising their own compositions.

All of this continues to hold true for pupils as they move into secondary schooling, particularly if they lack experience of composing. There are, however, changes in learning needs during the later middle years which arguably support the inclusion of work in small groups, with perhaps three to five participants. One of the most obvious of these comes with the shift of musical interest towards polyphonic textures, harmonically based or otherwise, which simply demand more singers or players. Most pupils up to the age of 14 and beyond still require a large proportion of their musical 'workings-out' to take place in action, through improvising and a certain amount of trial and error. These requirements can be met through work on keyboards, particularly those with memory and multi-tracking facilities, or by using composing software on computer. Compositions can either be designed for these media or can be drafted and then tried out with other performers later. This is a realistic model, though it requires a generously resourced school setting to achieve, and pupil time which extends beyond the usual lesson allocations.

For some students, working with a group, playing or singing together from the outset is preferable at this stage, either for musical or social reasons. Pragmatically, it is likely that most music composed for live group performance will need to be evolved at least partly through live work with the players. It is only by trying out and listening, composing the music so that it can be realistically played, and hearing the combined effect, that music involving more than one part can evolve to the point where it is ready for performance. Group work that is initiated for this purpose can be organised on two different bases. It may be that an individual still holds the composing role, with the remainder of the group subject to direction or offering ideas that can be taken or left. Alternatively, the group can act as joint composers, collaborating creatively throughout the making process. This way of working may be justified as a useful learning tool for young composers or it may be recognised as a composing model in itself.

The question therefore arises of where, in adult musical practices, to find the models of composing as a collaborative process. The lone composer has plenty of recognisable images: the 'great composer', the singer song-writer and so on. Collaborative composing is less visible. Nankivell identifies three broad categories of ways in which group composing works in the wider world of music:

a) adding new elements to already existing pieces, e.g. Inuit, Korean and the folk traditions;
b) between people of different levels of experience, status and, frequently, generation e.g. the Beatles and George Martin . . . ;
c) between colleagues of roughly equivalent status, e.g. . . . Lennon/McCartney, Fripp/Eno.

(Nankivell 1999a: 136)

Nankivell traces group composition as a composing approach, particularly in relation to contemporary popular music and argues that this is a process with plenty of models and potential for classroom application. He draws on the work of Ruth Finnegan who carried out an anthropological study of music-makers in an English town, Milton Keynes. By looking at composing over a complete cross-section of the population, Finnegan arrives at a useful classification of composing practices. She makes the distinction between 'prior written composition by an individual', the traditional 'classical' model, and 'composition-in-performance', which generally remains unwritten. The latter she found mainly practised by jazz and rock musicians, and not on the whole written down, except perhaps in outline. For the jazz musicians, this is improvisational composing, taking place both before and within performance. For the rock musicians, the music is mostly composed, but through a performance process. These are familiar distinctions of style, of course, but Finnegan highlights the extent to which ordinary citizens are involved in composing across the whole spectrum between these two basic processes. She also points out the great differences in the values attached to the different processes:

> In contrast to the widely recognised classical or (by now) jazz modes, the rock form has been virtually ignored in discussions of musical composition. And yet this form of composition is widely practised – composition which takes place in a gradual and, in a sense, collective manner through active and prior practice, resulting not in a written text but in a joint performance. It needs to be recognised as one authentic system in its own right, rather than somehow inferior to, or an unsuccessful copy of, classical or jazz compositional models.
>
> (Finnegan 1989: 173)

There is a need to reflect these distinctions in school, in ways that enable pupils to be aware of the stylistic contexts underpinning the working models and value each accordingly. The concomitant differences in the use of notation can also be recognised as stylistically based. Pupils are then able to work with the different process models as appropriate to the task in hand.

Nankivell pursues the 'composition-in-performance' approach into one particular classroom model of group composing. As discussed in Chapter 3, he suggests that group composing is often a two-stage process, with members of the group taking different roles. One individual brings an initial idea, words, melody or harmonic outline, for example, which the rest will arrange, contributing their own creative input on the way. So within a group project pupils may work on their ideas together from the outset or they may take the initial musical ideas from one group member or the teacher. Bands who work in this way have an ongoing relationship as a group, working together through series of compositions, and this can also be considered in planning group composing.

The model of a class working in groups on a composing task is one frequently found in middle and secondary schools, or primary schools where music is taught as a weekly class run by a teacher other than the class teacher. Often, however, this is a purely organisational device, used as a way of managing composing activities for a whole class of pupils in a short space of time, with any rationale beyond this left rather vague. Even for pupils old enough and socially skilled enough to co-operate satisfactorily, this can lead to poor quality work, with little sense of direction and only a token outcome at the end. It is not an easy situation to manage, given the hazards of noise and the difficulties of supervision and keeping pupils on task (Gilbert 1995). If pupils are to compose successfully in groups, both teacher and class must be clear about both the musical and educational reasons for doing so. In addition, the roles of group participants and the different working processes to be used need clarification and review as part of the whole enterprise.

The views of adolescent pupils on group composing have been investigated by Odam and Paterson (1999) as part of much wider project on composing in the secondary classroom. In a large survey (864 respondents) the majority of pupils between the ages of 11 and 14 said they preferred working in groups to working alone. It is hard to know how much this stems from what they are used to, the need for a group to bolster confidence, a general sociability or a real musical need. From 14 to 16, well over half prefer and find it easier to work alone.

Improvising as a composing process

By the later middle years, pupils are in a position to become increasingly aware about the distinction between improvised and composed music and to move between these two modes of music-making in different ways. Quite apart from its essential value as a creative musical process in its own right, improvising becomes part of a more complex relationship with composing. Drawing the distinction from the way in which it emerges in young children's music-making, this can be taken broadly as separating improvised music – 'made as played or sung' – from composed music which is returned to in stages, with time for reflection and alteration, and 'fixed' as a final, recoverable form, a 'composement' (Chapter 5). Given the need, noted earlier, for composing still to be based pragmatically in 'hands-on' and 'ears-on' work, with instruments and performers gathered together, improvisation is clearly quite strategic in relation to composing outcomes. Just as pupils can be expected to have some awareness of the different processes involved in group composing, enabling appropriate means to be employed, so they can explore explicitly the relationships between improvising and composing within their own working methods.

Burnard proposes this kind of metacognitive approach as part of the conclusions she draws from a research study looking at 12 year old children's experience of musical improvisation and composition. She suggests:

> teaching improvisation and composition should incorporate: i) examining past and present assumptions about what it is to improvise and compose; ii) encouraging children to be more reflective by asking children to think about *how* as well as *what* they improvise and compose.
>
> (Burnard 2000a)

Burnard's study gives interesting insights into children's perceptions of the two processes. She categorises children's experiences of the relationship between improvising and composing as taking three forms:

1 Improvisation and composition as ends in themselves and differently orientated activities;
2 Improvisation and composition as interrelated entities whereby improvisation is used in the service of making and performing a composition;
3 Improvisation and composition as indistinguishable forms that are inseparable in intention.

(Burnard 2000a)

These are reflections of the different ways pupils work and have interesting resonance against the music of much younger children at the point where improvising and composing divide. One of the factors that comes through Burnard's work strongly is the diversity in the ways children both use and perceive these different creative processes. This is another strong argument for teachers working in ways which allow such differences to be uncovered and acknowledged. This is partly a matter of how pupils understand what they are doing, and are therefore given control over the processes of their own composing. It is also, however, an issue of which working processes suit which individual children as composers.

> S and J (11 years) spend several after-school sessions improvising together on their chosen instruments: a guitar and a pair of conga drums. To begin with this is a purely recreational activity, fuelled by the enjoyment of working in a room, by themselves, at the end of the school day and in circumstances in which they can hear themselves think. Either during a session, or perhaps reflecting on the music by himself, J had come up with a chord progression which he thought would make the basis for a piece. During the next two sessions, J composes music for the two to play together, instructing S what to do. In the next session, the music is performed for some friends, brought along to listen.

In this case, the compositional ideas seem to have come as a result of the improvisation, though without any initial intent for this to happen. Here improvising is invaluable as a way of becoming immersed in the sounds and feel of the possibilities of this particular performing and instrumental relationship, without having to work towards anything beyond an immediate musical result. Inhabiting the medium in a free and unpressured way stimulates the composing imagination to get to work on the musical images experienced. This is a commonplace musical scenario, and yet in terms of provision for composing in the main curriculum, such unstructured beginnings find little room, not least because there are no guaranteed outcomes.

At a deeper level, Burnard uncovers subtle relationships between what she terms 'bodily intention' in the physical use of instruments and the processes of improvising and composing. From the study discussed above, she found that children's choice of instruments for improvising were characterised by 'an overwhelming preference for percussion instruments over keyboard or orchestral instruments', despite the fact that many of the pupils had tuition and had passed grade exams on the latter.

> The main advantage of percussion instruments was: to reduce the need for specialist skills and specific techniques, to allow kinaesthetic response; to orient towards continuity by allowing the body to feel, hear and think simultaneously; to ensure continuity of action; and enhance communicative dialogue and interaction between players.
>
> (Burnard 1999b)

When composing, however, it was prior instrumental experience that was helpful. In this context, children were able to use their already acquired performance skills and improvising became a stage on the way to composing, characterised as 'playing around'. 'In this way they accessed a well-spring of

existing ideas using known movement patterns already encoded in the kinaesthetic memory' (ibid.). And, as seen earlier, this memory has stylistic roots.
That the physical interaction with the instrument moves into a different relationship with the musical outcome in these different creative processes, is a
dimension to be taken into account when listening to pupils' work. It is interesting to note that, when improvising, students feel they need a margin of
technical safety. They choose instruments which are, rightly or wrongly,
perceived as simpler to play and which allow them to enter with more security
into the freedom of music-making in which they don't know what will happen
next. There may also be an overlay of association with notated compositions.
Instruments they choose come with written music to depend on. Departing
from the notation is in itself a big step. These instruments, however, associate
themselves for this very reason with ready-made pieces to play. Helping
students to cross these boundaries, in both directions, can enrich the scope for
both improvisation and composition across a wider palette of possibilities.

Whatever the compositional processes engaged in, the issue of style needs
to be recognised in one last area of children's work during the later middle
years. Once the music is made, thought has to be given to finding appropriate
media for saving work, and to the process of realisation in performance, either
for recording or for a live audience. In this respect, stylistic differences can be
allowed for in determining how things are done. By this stage, teachers have
an eye to pupils' participation in adult musical settings, and composers should
be allowed to see their work through to performance accordingly. This often
becomes an issue of time, but the benefits of giving time to the final stages of
musical realisation far outweigh the cost. Time spent composing, and the quality of the outcome, should be endorsed by valuing the music enough to
produce it well. Going through the full process is motivating in itself, as pupils'
confidence grows and they begin to see how their music can be communicated
to others.

For some music, notating a written version will be the first stage, either in
manuscript or with the aid of computer software. Learning even the beginnings of how to score music effectively and using appropriate conventions of
staff, graphic or other notations is an important composing tool. This is borne
out if other performers are then required to learn and rehearse the music from
a score. In other music, the piece remains unwritten, or can be saved on disc.
In all cases, a rehearsal stage is essential, continuing after the composition is
complete, when attention shifts to the performing issues of tempo, balance,
good ensemble, technical accuracy and musical interpretation, as well as
projection and stage presentation, if needed. Composers may have to learn
how to rehearse their music with other performers, conveying the effect they
want. Pupils can be expected to record their music and, if facilities are available to do this, to do so with some understanding of the positioning of mikes,
multi-track recording, and so on. In presenting work to an audience, learning
about 'stage' positioning, starts and finishes, introductions and acknowledge-

ment of applause all help to secure a sense of achievement in allowing the musical quality to be heard.

For some pupils, these are the last encounters they will have with music in a school situation. It is important that they move on equipped to present their music, with confidence enough to know that they can let their compositions be shared with a wider audience.

Chapter 8

Composers in education

One of the dilemmas running through the discussions in this book is that of how children's work in composing connects with the wider world of music outside school. Projects through which professional composers are brought together with children to compose music are now becoming increasingly available to schools. In the UK, there is often a generous amount of funding available for such projects through the Performing Rights Society (PRS), in conjunction with local education authorities, arts centres or concert series, or through the education outreach work of opera companies, orchestras, and so on. Such initiatives are to be welcomed, and the experiences gained by the young participants, as well as by teachers and composers, can be of outstanding value: visionary, exciting, and unforgettable in the best of senses. Sometimes, however, the musical and educational value is reduced because such projects can be a minefield of misunderstandings. Communication between teachers and artists is not always straightforward. The skills required to create rich and positive learning situations, and the inherent complexities of the task, are not always fully recognised by the artists. Moreover, teachers are not always clear about how best to support the visiting composer, or how to contextualise the work for the children. This chapter looks at some of the issues concerning this kind of work, its benefits and hazards.

Artists in schools

The Calouste Gulbenkian Report *The Arts in Schools* included in its recommendations that:

> Special provision should be made by arts funding organisations and Local Education Authorities together to help prepare professional artists to work in schools.
> Schools should recognise the mutual benefits of working contacts between children, teachers and artists and should encourage visits and joint projects.
> Schools and artists should be matched with care, and detailed preparation and follow-up should be seen as essential elements of such projects.

> The importance of quality rather than quantity of contact should be recognised and in recognition of this close attention should be given to the evaluation of current schemes involving artists in education.
>
> (Gulbenkian 1982: 144, 17–20)

One of the things that comes through most clearly in the passages of this report is the concern to ensure that the quality of the educational experience for pupils, and for their teachers and the artists themselves, matches the high potential value of such collaborations. The recognition that artists need preparation, that they are not trained as teachers, 'nor is education their major professional concern' (ibid.: 114, para 186) leads to a concern for the provision of some kind of preparation or training which is still widely lacking. The report endorses the value of artists-in-education projects for a number of reasons. Alongside the obvious benefits for pupils and teachers of an input from a highly specialised professional whose skills and imagination can extend the range of what the curriculum offers, there is also a belief in the importance for young people of contact with artists for whom art, music, dance and so on are professional work and not just leisure activity. This helps both to demystify the arts and to emphasise the seriousness of artistic endeavour, possibly affecting children's attitudes to the arts:

> The arts, like many other things in schools, can seem to pupils to be remote from the concerns and interests of everyday life. This remoteness can be reinforced where they are taught only about particular works of art and gain no understanding of the personal processes – of commitment, effort, and achievement – by which men and women have created them.
>
> (Gulbenkian 1992: 117, para. 193)

Certainly, this can be the case with music. A long history in music education at every level has been centred on the study of musical 'works', with the working processes of the men and women who composed them often very peripheral or even deemed completely irrelevant. 'I liked your music. You are the first composer I have ever seen.' wrote one youngster to the composer after a project. Asked about their picture of a composer, 9 and 10 year olds volunteered some further descriptions:

> They look like normal people but they have a feeling for music. They might be a bit strict with the music . . . they play it how they want it to be played and if someone else comes along and plays it wrong, they'll get really mad.

> They'd be able to play loads of instruments because they test out their music. They'd have loads of paper all over the floor, and pens and pieces of paper and ideas and things. They're probably quite messy, but quite posh as well.

> Someone with grey hair. They have a lot of time and they don't wear too posh clothes because they have to stay at home and work all the time.

If it was a pop group, like drum and bass, I would think of them in scruffy T-shirts and baggy trousers and things like that.

And a 7 year old added:

They're 60 or 70 because they have to get used to writing music first.

(Hunt 1999)

The importance of making composers visible is hard to exaggerate in relation to children's understanding of musical composition and access to it for themselves. As these remarks indicate, children's ideas of composers are often somewhat fragile. Although it may be a shame to spoil their illusions, meeting actual composers opens a door onto what is so often a backstage process. From the composer's perspective, however, it is not always easy to know how to present what you do either. Performers going into classrooms can easily make an impact by the performance presentation in itself – the musical sound, the virtuoso skills, and the additional scope for livening up the show with hose-pipes for brass players, tin cans and dustbins for percussionists – all have an immediacy which is compelling. For composers who turn out to look like ordinary people, and at most perhaps have a CD of their own music to show, it is not until work is well underway that it begins to become clear how they do what they do.

The Performing Rights Society have as the criteria for assessment of their composer in education projects the following aims:

The PRS believes its composer membership is a special resource which should be used to
a) help with the development of composition skills in the classroom, both as regards GCSE and as a component of the National Curriculum,
b) advance music composition by and for all, and thereby to demystify the art of composition, not only for children, but also for their teachers, parents, school authorities and other youth leaders,
c) raise public perception of the composer and his/her music, to advance the cause of modern musics of all kinds, to raise the public perception of the PRS.

(Perkins 1998)

The Gulbenkian Report emphasises the value of composer in education projects for teachers, as a way of being kept up to date with developments in contemporary arts, whatever their personal skill levels or expertise. The report sees working alongside professional artists as an invaluable way to do this, given the lack of time for self-development in the normal course of teaching: 'There are two main ways in which these schemes can be of benefit to teachers: by broadening their range of personal and professional *contacts* and by providing valuable *material* for their own work in schools' (Gulbenkian 1992: 117, para. 195).

Winterson (1994), in a largely positive evaluation of London Sinfonietta projects, developed by Gillian Moore since 1983, notes that teachers can be uncertain of their role in such projects and that the ideal of a project acting as INSET for teachers is not always realised. Indeed, a few teachers appear to withdraw altogether. It is quite clear that often a project is conceived and decided on by the planners from the artistic end with little or no reference to teachers at all. The project 'theme' is determined by works in repertoire or chosen by the artists who are involved, composers or performers, but with no consultation with teachers even as to the needs of pupils. In such a situation it may be less than surprising if teachers take a step back and leave it to the artists to carry on, whether through lack of confidence or even interest. Since the teacher is always the pivot in such projects, a key to getting it right must be the maximum involvement of the teacher and a use of his or her expertise.

The question of starting points and project content can be a vexed one. The choice of composer will obviously determine some of the musical scope and direction. However, it may be considered that there will also be an onus on composers working in education to be open to widening their own scope in response to the pupils with whom they work. The Gulbenkian Report emphasises the importance of a good match of composers and projects with schools. Part of this is to see the needs of pupils as an essential part of the opening preparatory discussions and not something to be more or less expertly sensed on day one of a project by the artists arriving in school. Similarly, funding bodies and administrators with an overview of project provision from a number of different sources must take some responsibility for maintaining the kind of standards that would be applied in any educational context, such as equal opportunities provision. These issues arise in relation to representation of composers from different musical genres and styles, and from different ethnic backgrounds. PRS projects encompass an enormous range of musical styles and composers, male and female. The Children's Music Workshop, based in London, organises many different kinds of projects incorporating musicians into schools, and aims to reflect the cultural diversity represented in the school environment. (Blaber and Pountney 2000). A similar approach is needed where an education project is run by a single orchestra or opera company. In setting up an education department, as almost all now do, such an organisation has to take on board basic educational principles of equality and access, for instance, by representing the work of both male and female composers. This may impact on the running of the company as a whole.

Winterson traces the 'creative music workshop' approach used by orchestras and opera companies back to its roots in the 1970s when it was 'intended to give direct support to school teachers and to enhance music in the classroom . . . In the pioneering days of the 1970s and 1980s, the creative music workshop was developed by composer–teachers such as David Bedford and Nigel Osborne, who continue to generate new and exciting ideas in this field' (Winterson 1996: 265). Some of these earlier projects were run by composers and music educators in collaboration. By contrast, 'today's large-scale, high-profile projects mounted by orchestras appear to be developing into a full-scale industry on their own' (ibid.: 261). One of the problems here is that projects may be mounted for what are, from the educational point of view at least, the wrong reasons.

> According to a survey by the Arts Council of England (Hogarth *et al.* 1997), 78 per cent of all publicly funded arts organisations are involved with education work and 63 per cent have a dedicated education officer. There is a variety of models of organisation and of types of practice. These range from dedicated arts education organisations, such as theatre-in-education, to the appointment of a single education officer to an established arts organisation. At best education is fully integrated into the life and work of arts organisations, and is seen as a core function. At worst, it is a reluctant add-on: a minimal provision to meet funding requirements. As often, education is seen as important but peripheral to the main business of the organisation.
>
> (NACCCE 1999: 132)

Funding is often tied to being able to demonstrate that education is a part of the overall mission. The motivation supplied by the threat of falling audience numbers to try to recruit wider audiences, and the next generation, may not necessarily go far enough to sustain a real concern, backed by training and evaluation, to ensure a high quality of educational outcome. Tensions can result. One difficulty is that having a concert in a major venue at the end of a project may work well for the artists, but is not always the most effective model for the children participating. Winterson also highlights the problem in this kind of project of artists who lack communication skills or an understanding of how children learn. There is a real onus on education managers or project administrators to ensure that projects are staffed by those with appropriate skills and that all adults involved take roles which are appropriate to, and not beyond, their expertise.

A majority of composer-in-education projects take place on a much smaller scale, however, with a freelance composer working on a project with a single school or a small group of schools. At a general level, the potential benefits of this kind of contact between composers and children are many. Working alongside an expert, seeing how ideas are generated and handled, working through the different stages of the making process, solving compositional problems, and having their music listened to by a professional, are experiences which offer children something a school cannot achieve in any other way. In addition to these general benefits, each composer brings a particular musical style and working approach, which can introduce a new dimension to pupils' musical perceptions. The extent to which different aspects of this potential are realised depends on the type of project in question and how it is handled. Planning stages of such projects do not always address the issue of matching the type of project to the school situation and a frequent problem is that teachers are very little involved in the planning stages at all. Given the learning value of such projects when they work well, it is worth considering the range of possible approaches that could be adopted, and the composer's role within them. In all cases, what is crucial is how the project makes a contribution to pupils' composing development.

Project formats

Perhaps the most common form of composer-in-education project is that in which, after some initial planning meetings and INSET with teachers, a composer introduces a project in school from a pre-planned and agreed starting point. Children go on to compose their own music with the composer's help. For younger pupils this is usually done in groups. Several schools may be linked in the project and come together for a final concert at which all the music is performed. The starting point is obviously crucial. PRS projects demonstrate a wide variety of themes, often based on the kind of work the composer does, or linked to local places, events or community needs (Perkins 1998). These themes may be musical, such as an exploration of single line melodies, jazz modes or chord progressions; or they may be extra-musical, linked to a text, the work of a visual artist, a place or an historical event. The project theme acts as a starting point and the composing is the pupils' own, supported by the composer through a series of visits or sometimes a single day event.

On this model, the composer's role begins with arousing pupils' interest in the given starting point and then lending his or her skills to support the making process. This role has many permutations and, ideally, this is one of the areas for discussion between composers and teachers during the planning stage of a project. The extent to which the composer determines the musical beginnings, the way the composer interacts with pupils while work is in progress, and the kinds of feedback he or she gives are variables which can be considered and adapted to the situation in question. The ways in which the composer works gives pupils both a model of composing processes and practical help in developing an initial idea into a finished piece. The composer's expertise is used to facilitate the children's composing. Philip Cashian, a composer experienced in education projects, describes how he sees this role.

> You need to springboard off in the beginning. Then they start having ideas. They get to the point where they have a little bit of music from the ideas you've given them and then they won't know what to do with the music or how to stretch it. They'll write a little thing that lasts five seconds and think 'right, I've got to write something else now to go after it' – rather than thinking 'let's look at what we've got', and breaking it right down, looking at what it's made up of and thinking how they can expand it. So I get them to listen to what they've got rather than hearing it as one entity, breaking it down and see what it is that makes it interesting which makes you want to

go with it, and suggesting ways that we can expand it before we get to another idea. De-composing it is, I suppose, and then putting it back together and extending it. And it's always stretching it rather than adding something after. And that's just a technical trick. That's where you've got the skill and they haven't – yes, the experience, knowing.

Teachers, even those who are already composers, can learn as much from watching this kind of process at work as can the pupils participating. Skill is needed on the part of the composer to find the balance between enough input to allow some modelling to take place and too much, which may take away the pupils' sense of ownership. Nankivell highlights the imbalance in skill and experience between composer and pupils and links it to his model of group composing (see page 34-5). From his perspective as a composer in this kind of project Nankivell comments:

> The approach I take is that everyone has the capacity to invent material (a melody, a rhythm, a lyric etc.) and we can all do that successfully. However, certainly at the start of our compositional lives, we do not all have the skills in terms of how to arrange the invented material. These skills do not need to be highly honed, but can be ideas such as 'repeat it' or 'do it as a round' or 'add a riff' /ostinato as an accompaniment'. My skill as a collaborative composer is not in coming up with fantastic ideas for a piece; these can, and do, come from the class groups working with me. My skills are more in terms of suggesting ways to arrange, develop or extend ideas.
>
> (Nankivell 1999b: 3)

The roles of invention and arranging may fall to individuals or groups and there are many permutations of how the processes may be shared in any one situation. Nankivell's analysis gives the composer a clear role in relation to children's own creativity: to encourage and elicit their ideas within a receptive environment, and in relation to the ongoing development of the process skills required to work ideas into a composition. Here composers act as mentors who, in the early stages of work with less experienced or younger children, contribute their skills towards 'arranging' the initial ideas. The expectation is that a progression takes place as the composer enables pupils to learn to do this for themselves: 'as the children begin to understand how arrangements can work . . . they can gradually take control of how their group compositions are both invented and arranged' (Nankivell 1999a: 145). Pupils work towards becoming autonomous composers. Meanwhile the dialogue is two-way and so is the inspiration: 'I am often inspired by working with children's radical lyrical ideas, their quirky unrestrained melodies and their joyful approach to using rhythms' (Nankivell 1999b: 4)

A composer working in a school setting in this way is there on a different basis from a teacher. Clearly, the aim must be that the composer contributes in another way altogether. The immediacy of these encounters opens up unique opportunities for children to become caught up with the composer's feeling for music and its materials. Somehow, such a project should enable children to gain some first-hand insight into this particular composer's music and ways of working. Composing alongside a professional can go some way towards achieving the latter, especially if the composer is adept at letting the workings show in ways pupils can grasp. And this can be reinforced if there is time for reflection afterwards in a three-way conversation between composer, teacher and pupils. Such reflection is not just about pupils' work and what was learned and achieved, but about what they noticed about how the composer worked with the music too. Here the teacher is in a strategic position to elicit pupils' thoughts and make connections with ways of composing previously experienced. The teacher can also help pupils understand that different composers compose differently. This is an important contribution, particularly for older pupils who may be in the process of finding their own best ways of working.

Another project model involves a commission for a composer to write a piece for professional performance at the end of the project. The children's work is then linked to some aspect of the composer's piece, and their work is heard alongside the composer's music in the final concert, performed by themselves or in collaboration with the performers. In this format, one of the objectives is that pupils will gain a deeper insight into the work of a composer by, as it were, following in their footsteps, shadowing some aspect of how the piece has been put together, or exploring for themselves the starting point from which it came. This is an experience in itself, but it also strengthens understanding of someone else's music. As a general idea this is sound, but it can have pitfalls. It is dependent on the quality of the connection made between the children's project and the music itself and that this is well-judged in relation to pupils' interests and abilities. The most straightforward of such projects is perhaps those which borrow a medium – electro-acoustic music, for example – where the project leads children into new territory while leaving plenty of scope for working at different levels of complexity. The fact that it is the children accommodating themselves to the composer's perspective is both a strength and a hazard.

An issue arises in this kind of project over how and when pupils are introduced to the composer's music. Frequently, for financial and practical reasons, this happens only at the end of the project. Again, there are pros and cons. This may be a good thing because it avoids pupils feeling pressure either to imitate or to avoid doing so. It also prevents difficulties arising from pupils not liking the music, finding it difficult or alien. In theory, it enables pupils to listen from a basis of greater insight and understanding, although in the excitement over their own work, children are often in the least likely state to enter into someone else's. On the other hand, links with the composer's work may never become clear at all if there is no introduction to the music while there is still time for discussion.

A different kind of project brings composers into school, just to introduce and talk about their own work. Children can prepare questions they would like to ask and carry out an interview themselves. They can discover what the composer does, how they conjure up a piece of music and how they think about the decisions they have to take. Music can be introduced and investigated before the visit, stimulating more questions that need answering. Live demonstration by the composer of some of the workings-out adds more possibilities. Such a project is quite different in kind and obviously doesn't involve pupils so directly, but the learning potential can be considerable. If during their time in one school, children can meet several such visiting artists or even by means of videos, recordings and books begin investigating what composers say about their music, in relation to the sound of the music itself, a whole new perspective is opened up. Pupils can be encouraged to see that part of developing as a composer is that your ideas change and develop. They can learn how creative work involves not only imagination, but also risk and uncertainty and often very hard, painstaking work. Yet another type of project brings composers into a role perhaps closer to that of the teacher, in which children begin their own composing work first and the composer visits several times while work is in progress. An interesting variation on this was a project carried out in Cornwall by the composer Andrew Hugill, who started the project off by visiting schools and followed through its later stages via the internet, with pupils uploading and sending work in progress, in a form which all involved could access.

Preparation for projects

Given that the rationale for a composing-in-education project is always centred on enhancing children's learning, the quality of the learning experience must be in the foreground of planning. It is inescapable that, in almost all cases, quality is dependent on planning which starts from:

- the particular needs and range of prior learning and experience of the pupils involved
- the context of the work in relation to the current music curriculum being followed
- a project focus that is timely and appropriate for all participants.

Every project must begin its planning stages with dialogue between teachers, composers and the organisers concerned. This should not consist of teachers being told what the project will be, nor composers being left to guess at what the school situation has in store. Everyone has a perspective to bring to the planning and each is important.

More specifically, certain fundamental points need to be agreed on at the outset of any project.

1   How will the project relate to children's ongoing learning in music, and in particular to their current composition work?
    Is the intention that the project links into a programme of learning which the school has planned for? Or is the project to be a freestanding 'event'?

2   What kind of role will the composer take in the project?
Who initiates the ideas? How are they worked with? Will the composer direct the composing strongly in order to model some possibilities? Will the composer follow the children's ideas and help them develop their own music?

3   What is the role of the composer's own work in the project?
Is it intended that the children gain an understanding of how this composer works, hear some of her/his music? Will there be discussion with the composer how about she or he sets about composing? Or is the composer contributing as a visiting composition teacher, with a particular perspective to bring to the work?

4   If the composer's own work is to play a part in the project, and, for example, be heard professionally performed at some point, how will this be managed?
Will the composer's music be introduced to the children by the composer or prior to the project by the teacher? Will time be planned into the project for discussion and focus on the composer's way of working, perhaps to prepare children to listen to performances? What introduction will teachers have to the composer's music?

5   How is the role of teachers seen in each project?
How will the teacher's knowledge of pupils be used for planning preparatory and follow up work? How will the organisation and management roles be shared? Who will lead which aspects of the project?

6   How will the project be sequenced and what kind of an ending will it have?
Will there be a final concert? small or large-scale, for a single school or more? For parents or public? Will it include 'talk-back' between teachers, composers, audience? Will there be a professional performance of children's music? discussion between composers and performers? Will there be class-based sessions to listen to and record finished work?

7   Whatever the culminating event, how will the music and the experience be evaluated with the pupils?
Will this include self-assessment by pupils? By composers and teachers? Will it include discussion between composer, teacher and children? How much time is allowed for this?

Usually a training day is set up prior to the project. All too often, the assumption here is that this is for teachers to be trained by the composers and other project leaders. An INSET day can however be much more than composers running through 'what we'll be doing when we get there' or finding out what equipment the school has. If the day is based on truly collaborative work, this sets the tone for the whole project. Teachers must expect to contribute fully and composers must expect to use teachers' expertise. There needs to be a two-way process in which composers learn about the context they'll be working in and teachers learn about the composer's ideas and approach. From this, fine detail can be planned together.

The pupils too must be clear what is happening. They may or may not take part in the early planning but composers shouldn't be arriving without some preparations in the school. Pupils will need an introduction to the project personnel and their different roles and to the specific learning aims of the project in relation to their own composing, for example:

- to meet a professional performer/composer and be part of one of their compositions;
- to be helped by a professional composer to compose their own music;
- to meet a professional composer and find out how they work, or to try some of their ideas;
- to learn some composing techniques, such as setting words in song writing, exploring how amplified sound can be used in composing.

There can also be discussion with pupils of how the project will be useful for them as composers or how it will connect with what they've recently been working on.

This is a long agenda and needs time and co-operation from all if a project is to be fully successful. The importance of bringing children into contact with professional composers makes the effort it costs more than worthwhile. Such events can leave children with life-long memories and, if well managed, can fire a creative spark that can engender extraordinary work.

Chapter 9

Composing in schools

For children, as for anyone, composing is grounded in their own biographies and musical experiences. We have to recognise that music in school is only the smallest part of this. When we look at teaching and learning in composition, in the school setting, we have to see how it contributes to a much bigger picture beyond. It is no good imagining that school is the starting point, or even that it is the main source, of musical experience. The encounters children have through music in school are a piece only of a much wider whole. This does not mean, of course, that these encounters are unimportant. Indeed, school may be the one place where children find encouragement to make their own music. And schools can be central in giving children the tools, understanding and wider vision that allows their composing to reach beyond anything previously imagined.

Enabling this to happen depends on finding ways of making these very slight encounters – the times for music in school – genuinely meaningful occasions. For teachers try to do too much, under circumstances in which doing less is often doing more. This is so in several senses: trying to fit too many small pieces of work into the tiny amount of time available, and trying to take over too much of the composing which children are quite capable of doing for themselves. If we compress children's music, either by expecting it all to be crammed into a small amount of time, or by confining it too tightly with constraints of a set task, then we are in danger of losing its inner quality altogether.

One of the real challenges for teachers is to let children's music breathe, to allow enough space for the music to find its real shape and its real form and energy. Looking back over the music gathered during the study described in Chapter 3, I realised that much of the 'best' music had been composed on Wednesday afternoons. This was no coincidence, since it was a time in the week when children from all classes were able to choose from a range of activities set up all over the school. They could choose to work with a teacher or to manage their own activities, independently and in their own time. Although all the composing on this project was on a basis of choice and open access, it was on Wednesdays that pupils could find themselves a corner out of the way and, if they wanted to, spend the whole afternoon on the activity. And the difference was audible, although it is not easy to analyse. These opportunities allowed for really extended time frames, which meant that the music was more substantial and more 'lived in', often returned to time and again. Perhaps most noticeably, though, it was in the ideas *for* the music that the quality came through, giving it a vividness of character and impact that stood out among the rest. Similarly, it is often those pupils, particularly in secondary settings, who return day after day before or after school for time alone with a choice of instruments and somewhere to settle, who produce music that really grows and gathers an excitement of discovery as the weeks go by. Something begins to come through, as if they have become reconnected with their musical selves, and gradually the music starts to gain a new authenticity. Of course, pupils like these have selected themselves to take up the opportunities in a way that not all children will. But they have a surprising degree of influence among their peer group. Others begin to imitate and something new takes off.

The art for teachers, then, is in finding ways to manage composing inside schools in such a way as to generate musical quality in an atmosphere of creative discovery. In an encounter with a new class, particularly where composing has not featured much in the music curriculum previously, the best launching strategy is just to ask for a piece, ask for a song, or ask if anyone thinks they could make up some music, now or for next time. If this is a completely new thought for a class, or children look puzzled or less than enthusiastic, follow-up questions can be 'have you ever made any music of your own?', 'do you think it would be hard to compose your own music? . . . why?' or 'how do you think composers start to make a new piece?'. It is unlikely, however, that there won't be at least a few who will take up the challenge. All the teacher needs is one or two offers. Arrangements are made, the class holds its breath and somebody sings or plays, there and then, or at the next lesson or music time. And the listening begins. More likely still, it gradually comes to light that many of the pupils have relevant and useful experience already. They may not volunteer this information to start with and sometimes children aren't sure what composing really means or what would 'count'. But the wagon starts to roll and soon more jump aboard. What this strategy secures very effectively is the idea that pupils' own music is of interest, of value, and that someone wants to listen. This is where the teaching starts.

At this point, if teachers are also somewhat unsure, they may have to hold their nerve for a bit. The teacher of a class of 10 year olds, who had never composed in school and were not very 'keen on music', asked if anyone thought they could compose some music at home and bring it in. To her surprise quite a number took up the challenge and came back with their pieces, all songs, two or three of which were done on a home karaoke. The children had replaced the old words with new ones and sung along to the backing track. The class received these very well – this was real music – and the singers were given considerable applause. The teacher was less sure. Nevertheless, she talked about the music and encouraged the work to continue. After several copies of the same idea by other children, and just as the teacher was feeling that this, although clearly motivating, was going nowhere, someone had an idea. 'We could make up our own backing track!' This was the take-off point and the children began working out their own, newly composed songs. Being encouraged, having their early efforts taken seriously, and being allowed to stay with the idea was enough for them to reach the point where they had the confidence to go back to their own music-making. Once there is music being made, whatever it is, and however little it seems at the outset, the teacher can begin to work with it. From here on, the two-strand approach described in earlier chapters can begin.

This takes the form of organising the composing that takes place in school on a basis of two kinds of commissions. The first is the children's self-commissions, in which the teacher's role is initially just to encourage, although input may follow later. Children devise their own ideas for the kind of music they want to make, working towards their own musical purposes. These opportunities are crucial in sustaining children's compositional independence and sense of musical self. The second strand is that of the commissions given by the teacher. These may create a focus on music that explores a particular musical idea or technique. Here, the commissions offer structures and materials which can supply new concepts and composing tools. A good source for these is the fund of ideas that arise in children's own music and can be highlighted, explored and then used as the basis for a new composition. Other kinds of commissions may be related to particular events, music that is needed for dance or drama, music linked to a class music topic, or, particularly for older pupils, music for particular performers to sing or play.

Planning for these two strands works differently with different age groups. During the early years, self-commissions take the form of choosing music as a play activity, using whatever equipment is available, and 'planning' music prior to making it, using a 'plan–do–review' format or some simple alternative. Teacher commissions will need to be very open – 'could you make some music for this xylophone?', 'shall we make some turn-taking music' or 'would anyone like to make us a song?' – whilst other input runs alongside. The timing of both kinds of commission has to be fairly fluid, more in the nature of ongoing opportunities, semi-structured by the equipment available. As children move through primary school, they become increasingly able to respond to teacher commissions and the organisation for composing can alter accordingly. In many primary settings, flexibility for self-commissions can be maintained, with outcomes shared with the class in short sessions as needed. Teacher commissions can either find a place in a music session, or be initiated in the session but carried out flexibly in between times. In middle and secondary schools, music becomes confined to timetabled slots, but it becomes increasingly realistic to expect homework and to provide for extra-curricular or after-school club top-up. It remains important, however, to sustain the two kinds of work.

Where curriculum planning is expected to be tightly organised into medium term units – half a term's work, say – there is clearly some tension in relation to these ways of working. This becomes greater as the children become older. In particular, if opportunities for self-commissions are to be flexible but consistent, this needs either to be planned as a separate ongoing strand with adaptable time-frames, or as intermittent 'content-free' units which can alternate with units containing teacher commissions. Another option is to allow pupils to opt out of set units in order to do their own composing. This can be organised on a rolling programme so that through the year each pupil has at least one or two such opportunities. A deeper conflict arises in how to enable planning of input to be at least partly led by what comes out of pupils' own work and their immediate needs for specific techniques and understanding. With adaptable planning frameworks, a balance can be achieved. Pre-planned inputs which introduce new areas for investigation, including work linked to music of different times and places or particular styles and genres, can be adapted as necessary to suit the current concerns in a particular class. Any unit involving composing should allow enough time for the composing to be completed with some quality. Being realistic about the stages of work involved if this is to be achieved is a key to avoiding the kind of compressed activity referred to earlier.

Thinking through the processes of composing and how work develops over a year, flexibility is needed on another front as well. The stages gone through in producing a composition will include some or all of:

- devising an idea for some music, finding a starting point, researching the demands of context and purpose
- composing the music, moving through the processes of exploration, drafting, developing, refining and fixing
- rehearsing the music, working on the performing aspects, possibly with other singers or players, reaching a standard for presentation
- saving the music: recording, notating, or saving on disc
- performing or presenting the music to an audience, or making the work available for listening in other ways
- reflecting on the music and composing processes, during and after work in progress; evaluating your own composing.

On any real time-scale, it is clear that this is often quite a long process. Apart from the youngest pupils for whom 'now ' is all there is, any composing which aims at quality across even several, if not all of these stages, is going to require work over time. How many such pieces of work will fit into a year? This greatly depends on the extent to which composing reaches beyond class time. If there is flexibility for projects by different pupils to overlap, to have different time spans, and even for more than one piece to be on the go at the same time, the staging of work towards a finished piece can be seen through to its musical conclusion. For one pupil, three or four such pieces may be a year's work, for another perhaps more. Once a week, quick, composing explorations within one music lesson need to be seen in another category of work altogether. Each pupil can then look back and identify a core of finished compositions, known inside out, lived with, heard and listened to, thought about, recognised by other people and enjoyed. And some of these will be performed in concert or kept in the class listening or performing repertoire.

Recognising difference becomes a musical necessity. In the adult world, amateur or professional, no composer composes in every style, even if they have the facility, no musician plays every instrument, and people go through periods of interest in a particular musical field and then move on. Children should be able to focus their work in a similar way. Although there is no doubt a responsibility in music education to widen perspectives and open up new avenues, this needs to be combined with provision for some 'specialisation' if we are to avoid disabling children musically by disconnecting them from what they are good at. For the youngest children, a period of interest in a favourite instrument, or a phase of song-making, is like a craze on a particular game or play activity. Allowing it to run its course enables the child to make progress and secure some learning. As children learn instruments and gather performing skills, their composition may capitalise on these. In this case, there is a distinctive range of composers in the class which stems from stylistic and cultural differences, differences of musical focus – for instance, between single line and polyphonic instruments – differences of ensembles, and differences in performing opportunities. Pupils who have a strength or interest in technology may base their composing in this, either as a tool or as a composing medium in itself, without need for performers. Somehow, these need to co-exist, as part of the whole picture. Quite apart from the practicalities, this, too, raises issues of curriculum planning. We tend to expect that each child will follow the same programme of work. To what degree is it acceptable for difference to make a difference? It has been argued in Chapter 6 that, if composing is to develop with any depth, it is essential for pupils to take different pathways. Translated into curriculum planning terms, how far can this be taken?

If we are to sustain any vision of how composing can be at its best in schools, we need to consider at a practical level what it is that can really make a difference to the quality of pupils' work. No situation is ideal, and compromises have constantly to be made. Without some sense of what provision would be ideal, however, even the small improvements that are possible never come about. The following sections focus on some of the areas of practical provision which can be considered if such improvements are being looked for. The underlying question here though, is what, within a school setting, makes for high quality composing? What is it that, even in a small way, can really make a difference? If the answers to these questions are lost sight of, the whole enterprise can become sadly drained of life.

Time

The importance of making flexible amounts of time available for composing is a constant theme. Time that is spacious and undisturbed allows pupils to be immersed in their work, to lose themselves in it and so to find their musical bearings. Being able to choose when time is taken for music can also be a key factor. Short periods of quality time, with thinking spaces in between, can be an effective pattern for some. Time away from the classroom is available to everyone, if pupils are motivated to use it. And sometimes, the pressure of having to come up with the music in a short time can be just what is needed to spur on ideas. Altogether, time is very subjective in relation to creative work, and it is needed in variable amounts. The fact to be faced is that music has to be heard in time, so that all processes of experimenting, assembling, trying out, listening to and reviewing music have an added time factor that can't be dispensed with.

Quiet

Quiet is needed for sensitive listening and for undisturbed work. Most music, but particularly that which is itself quiet, subtle, and colourful in timbre, needs a clean sound space in which to be heard. This is the equivalent of the clean sheet of paper in art that offers the space in which marks are made. Children who are learning to listen must be able to hear the sound marks they are making. They can also learn to make and use silence musically, understanding how it can feel differently charged, depending on context and how it is precipitated. And contrary to impressions, if the surroundings are quiet, much of children's music-making will itself be fairly unobtrusive. It can be useful to maintain the traditional distinction between quiet and loud instruments and to provide differently for each. Some musics, most obviously drumming ensembles and rock groups, need to be loud and the quality is reduced if this isn't possible. These need a form of provision in which they are exiled from ordinary working situations, but given the freedom they require at certain times. With some technologies, working with headphones allows pupils to work in privacy and enables work to be contained in its own sound space.

Materials

Voices come with the children. For the rest, instruments and technology, the materials for producing the rich palette of sound with which children can work, contribute to the quality of the music at a fundamental level. In defining much, though not all, of the sound world available, these lay out the range and limits of musical possibilities in a way that is of more than trivial importance. The collection of instruments in school offers the breadth of timbres, of materials – wood, metal, strings, and skins – of pitch, dynamic range and playing techniques, and of electro-acoustic sound, which significantly affects the sound of children's music. Even the provision of a range of beaters for percussion instruments immediately increases the scope for sensitivity and discrimination. Young children's music is profoundly affected by the sound, visual layout and technique of any instrument. If a collection of instruments is of quality in itself, beautifully made and maintained, it becomes enticing and irresistible to children as composers. Instruments with different world music roots bring immediately to the classroom something of their origins. Bass guitars and drum machines transform music for older primary children, since instruments also delineate the musical styles in which pupils can work convincingly. Keyboards, computers and sequencers bring composer and performer together and offer a dialogue in the composing process between the composer as listener and the composer as creator. The quality of equipment for recording and listening defines what pupils hear of their work once the activity of making it is over. For children with disabilities, adaptations of instruments can make the whole difference between being able to access the sound and not. Materials are not everything, but those there are have a profound impact on composing outcomes.

Aloneness

The opportunity for some creative aloneness with music is to be seen as essential for the youngest children and important for most children. Group traditions of performance sometimes dominate organisation for composing. Composing alone can be seen as both a creative need and a learning process. It is not until a child has all the control in his or her hands, so to speak, that both aurally and kinaesthetically the feeling of making the music comes fully home. The freedom to take flight in an improvisation, unchecked by anyone else, or to find out a musical idea, re-run it, transform, repeat, and work over something in your own time, alone, allows a train of thought to develop and find its own shape. Composing individually by using others as performers can also be seen as aloneness in the creative sense. The performers become the medium to be worked with in a way parallel to that in which a choreographer might work 'on the body' in creating dance.

Partnership

The need for aloneness doesn't detract in any way from the quite different opportunities offered by the interaction musically with someone else. Working in twos sets up musical possibilities that are importantly different from working alone or in a group. One-to-one encounters allow children to improvise music that plays out the kind of conversational interactions found in linguistic exchange, but with the additional dimension of being able to both 'talk' at once. The direct response to someone else, and the opportunity to join in with them in making a stream of music coherently, are manageable even for very young children working in pairs. And even young children who don't speak at all in school are sometimes able to form musical partnerships with another child or adult. Improvising, and later composing, in twos is where musical interaction develops. Musical understandings are developed from inside the music in a negotiation between the two participants that is wordless. For many children this is extremely significant and it also opens up an untranslatable musical consciousness. Importantly too, the musical consequences of such interactions are the most fundamental music structures on which composing is built: exchange, turn-taking, following-on from, transforming, the same thing at different times, passing, catching or dropping ideas, interlocking patterns, and ideas that fit together are all accessible. These are the building blocks of composing. Partnering children in music-making is also a key teaching strategy because of its musical scope and the potential for wordless interaction and negotiation of ideas. Traditionally, in many contexts, skills are passed from the experienced to the novice in this way.

Groupwork

Groupwork in composing has different meanings for children of different ages. Making music in groups spontaneously is part of the innate musical behaviour of pre-school children. The ability to find some group coherence in improvised music-making can find expression in any human group and any setting. Beyond the immediacy of improvisation, young children composing in groups often compose alone, though side by side. As children develop musically, working in groups offers, in developmentally related stages, the experience of mixed timbres and textures, rhythmic coherence, music layered in pitch and latest of all, harmony. The unfolding of these musical possibilities becomes a composing agenda in itself. For adolescent children, working together may have a supportive value in relation to confidence in a composing role. At the same time, composing which is done co-operatively by performing groups can allow ensemble music to be made that reflects the group roles found across different musical styles: rhythm or continuo sections, bass riffs or grounds, a consort of like instruments spread across the pitch range, or a vocal harmony texture. Recognising the musical opportunities arising from composing in groups promotes quality; dividing classes into groups with no musical rationale can diminish it.

Class community

The class, as a community of composers, provides the cohesion that enables individual work of any kind to flourish. The more room there is for diversity, the more the class as a musical community can thrive, because there is a constant stream of ideas and approaches for individuals to try out, exchange and build on. Organising the class community so that it is a forum to which music composed by any of its members can be brought is a powerful strategy. The reciprocal roles of listening and being listened to and of giving and receiving respect for musical endeavours increase both confidence and musical awareness. Knowing that work can be tried out with an audience contributes to the development of the inner sense of audience which composing needs. Listening together, to compositions by pupils or by others, builds a basis for the ongoing critical reflection on music that is also a key in composing development. Class composing histories often include periods of work when music by an individual or group becomes taken up by others, as everyone tries out a new-found idea. And creative risks can sometimes be taken because of the sense that at some level the work is shared, even when it is composed by one child alone.

Notebooks

Composing notebooks give pupils a place for reflection and allow the tracking of composing work. This gives both child and teacher a sense of the progression which is unfolding. Once children are old enough to use them with some enjoyment and not as a chore, they find satisfaction in seeing a record of work, and a composing biography, take shape. Reflecting on music made and planning future composing enterprises can connect past and future with a feeling of purpose and ongoing quest. This allows children's work to be heard and seen as part of a series of work, rather than as isolated events that are heard and forgotten. Discs, tapes and notations are kept alongside and indexed if necessary. Drawings, sketches of music, plans for pieces and reviews of music heard make a resource for future music-making. Notebooks can be taken on to the next class, helping to make continuity more easily achievable.

Reviews

If notebooks supply the means of collecting and tracking developing musical ideas and achievements, reviews with a teacher or with a peer, help children to recognise the progression that has taken place. Composing can never be assessed from a single piece of music in isolation. Standing back and taking the long view is important. For older pupils, the view can be across a year or a term; for younger children it may be much shorter. Assessment will take place anyway, but it is the opportunity to focus on the overview which helps pupils to think of change and moving forward that contributes an extra dimension in quality. Talking through the composing that has been done, and reviewing how it has developed can be encouraging in itself. Reviews that help make explicit the understanding of what has been achieved considerably raise the quality of the work done in school. They also make sure that music made is acknowledged and taken seriously.

Audience

Finally, we come back to the importance of enabling children's music to be heard. Finding an audience, people gathered together to listen, makes a crucial contribution to children's composing development. For most children, learning to prepare and present music for an audience helps them to engage with the questions of how their music is heard by others and how it communicates. Experience of listening from an audience point of view increases their understanding of the impact and effect their music has on those who listen to it. Some children may prefer their music to remain private and personal and this is to be respected. For those who are ready, however, audiences can be found in many settings and at different levels of formality. Sharing music with a friend, a group or a listening adult is a first step. Rehearsing and presenting music in concert, in school or for invited parents, may be the next. Children can be challenged to produce music for any ready purpose or occasion that also finds it an audience: plays, celebrations or assemblies, for example. Once children realise that their music is valued, not just as curriculum 'work', but to be heard and enjoyed by a wider audience, another dimension of quality opens up.

More experienced pupils can compose music for different performing groups in school. Choirs, recorders and other singing or instrumental groups should include children's compositions in their performing repertoire. Composing done in class or in extra-curricular composing 'clubs' can be included in school concerts; technology-based compositions can be presented on tape. Whole programmes of young composers' work across different age groups can make an excellent contribution to a year's concert calendar, in school or in a local arts venue. CD collections of children's music are now easy to make and distribute. If large ensembles such as steel bands, jazz bands and orchestra are too complex, pupils can compose for smaller groups of players drawn from these and their work included in concert programming in school or at the local music centre. Rock and pop bands can group together for performances in which their own material forms a substantial part of each set. Older pupils can compose music for younger children in their own or other schools to listen to or perform, and all pupils can be encouraged to compose for private and community occasions outside school altogether. Any of these strategies can help children's music to find its place in the wider community alongside other kinds of musical and creative activity. All this increases adults' understanding of what children's music has to offer.

The continuity of pupils' experience of composing in school is one of the major concerns underlying this book. I do not believe we have yet begun to see what the majority of children are capable of as composers. Observations in earlier chapters are based on the work of hundreds of children, carried out in many different contexts. Yet, for a majority of pupils of any age, the composing they are doing in school is often still in early stages. Too frequently, they have worked consistently for a year or perhaps two and then circumstances of one kind or another have intervened and the thread of continuity is lost. At each change of phase, or of school or even teacher, there is a tendency to treat a whole class as beginners and 'start again'. Opportunities to sustain consistent work across each phase of schooling are scant.

If the music-making children do outside school is ignored, it becomes a separate musical life. And if this happens, music in school loses its wider musical credibility. For it is the music made outside school which will be the lasting and real composing base, not the fragmented work produced within. There may be plenty of scope to enhance the quality of children's learning simply by revisiting questions of the way provision is organised and the expectations and frameworks within which it is managed. Sustaining opportunities and allowing children to work to the levels of which they are capable enables their composing to become an audible force in school music. Above all, it is necessary to continue to question and to try new approaches. There is far more uncharted territory in terms of pupil development than we might like to think, and composing in schools takes place in the context of much wider cultural and musical forces which have impact on children's work. Time spent on identifying what is to be aimed for may seem like idealism when viewed from some perspectives. Without such idealism, children's music is easily lost.

References

Addessi, A. R., Baroni, M., Luzzi, C. and Tafuri, J. (1995) 'The development of musical stylistic competence in children' *Bulletin of the Council for Research in Music Education* 127, *Special Issue 15th ISME International Research Seminar.*

Ash, B. and Rapaport, B. (1957) *Creative Work in the Junior School*, London: Methuen.

Bamberger, J. (1991) *The Mind Behind the Musical Ear*, Cambridge, Mass.: Harvard University Press.

Barrett, M. (1996) 'Children's aesthetic decision-making: an analysis of children's musical discourse as composers' *International Journal of Music Education* 28, 37–62.

—— (1997) 'Invented notations: a view of young children's musical thinking' *Research Studies in Music Education* 8.

—— (1998) 'Researching children's compositional processes and products' in Sundin, B., McPherson, G. and Folkestad, G. (eds), *Children Composing*, Malmö: Malmö Academy of Music, Lunds University.

Blaber, A. and Pountney, J. (2000) 'Children's Music Workshop: tenth anniversary' *Primary Music Today* 16.

Bruner, J. (1990) *Acts of Meaning*, Cambridge, Mass.: Harvard University Press.

Bunting, R. (ed.) (1975) *Personal – Practical – Topical: Some New Approaches to Examination Music*, Schools Council Project: Music in the Secondary School Curriculum Working Paper 2. York: University of York.

—— (1977) *The Common Language of Music*, Schools Council Project: Music in the Secondary School Curriculum Working Paper 6, York: University of York.

—— (1987) 'Composing music: case studies in the teaching and learning process' *British Journal of Music Education* 4.1, 25–52.

——. (1988) 'Composing music: case studies in the teaching and learning process' *British Journal of Music Education* 5.3, 269–310.

Burnard, P. (1999a) *'Into Different Worlds': Children's Experience of Musical Improvisation and Composition*, Ph.D. thesis: University of Reading, England.

—— (2000) 'How children ascribe meaning to improvisation and composition: rethinking pedagogy in music education' *Music Education Research* 2.1, 7–23.

—— (1999b) 'Bodily intention in children's improvisation and composition' *Psychology of Music* 27.2, 159–74

Burke, C. (1996) 'The Hope Valley Squeeze Box Project' *Primary Music Today* 6, Hebden Bridge: Peacock.

Cage, J. (1939/78) *Silence*, London: Marion Boyars.

C. Gulbenkian Foundation (1982) *The Arts in Schools*, London: Calouste Gulbenkian Foundation.

Castell, K. C. (1982) 'Children's sensitivity to stylistic differences in "classical" and "popular" music' *Psychology of Music, Special Issue*, 22–5.

Coleman, S. N. (1922) *Creative Music for Children*, New York: G. P. Puttnam.

Cook, N. (1998) *Music: A Very Short Introduction*, Oxford: Oxford University Press.

Cox, G. (1997) '"Changing the Face of School Music": Walford Davies, the gramophone and the Radio' *British Journal of Music Education* 14.1, 45–56. '

Czerniewska, P. (1988) The National Writing Project: reflections on writing' *Times Educational Supplement*, 4 March.

Davies, C. (1986) 'Say it till a song comes: reflections on songs invented by children 3–13' *British Journal of Music Education* 3.3, 279–94.

—— (1992) '"Listen to my song": a study of songs invented by children aged from 5 to 7 years' *British Journal of Music Education* 9.1, 19–48.

Deliege, I. and Sloboda, J. (eds) *Musical Beginnings*, Oxford: Oxford University Press.

DeLorenzo, L. (1989) 'A field study of sixth grade students' creative music problem-solving processes' *Journal of Research in Music Education* 37. 3, 188–200.

DES (Department for Education and Science) (1967) *Children and their Primary Schools*. A Report of the Central Advisory Council for Education (England), chaired by Lady Plowden, London: HMSO.

Dufallo, R. (1989) *Trackings:Composers Speak with Richard Dufallo*, Oxford: Oxford University Press.

Finnegan, R. (1989) *The Hidden Musicians*, Cambridge: Cambridge University Press.

Flash, L. (1990) 'Changing perceptions of music with reception children' *British Journal of Music Education* 7.1, 43–66.

Foley, J. R. (1978) 'Observing the nature of young children's musicality: an observation study of two classes in the center for young children' seminar paper, MENC, University of Maryland.

Folkestad, G., Hargreaves, D. and Lindström, B. (1998) 'Compositional strategies in computer-based music making' *British Journal of Music Education* 15.1, 83–98.

—— (1998) 'Musical learning as cultural practice: as exemplified in computer-based creative music making' in Sundin, B., McPherson, G. and Folkestad, G. (eds) *Children Composing*, Malmö: Malmö Academy of Music, Lunds University..

Gamble, T. (1984) 'Imagination and understanding in the music curriculum' *British Journal of Music Education* 1.1, 7–25.

Gardner, H. (1973) *The Arts and Human Development*, New York: John Wiley.

—— (1973a) 'Children's sensitivity to musical styles' *Merrill Palmer Quarterly of Behavioural Development* 19, 67–77.

—— (1984/93) *Frames of Mind* (2nd edn), London: Fontana.

Glynne-Jones, M. (1974) *Schooling in the Middle Years: Music*, London: Macmillan.

Glover, J. (1990) 'Understanding children's musical understanding' *British Journal of Music Education* 7.3, 257–62.

Glover, J. and Ward, S. (1998) *Teaching Music in the Primary School* (2nd edn). London: Cassell.

Glover, J. and Young, S. (1999) *Primary Music: Later Years*, London: Falmer.

Gilbert, R. (1995) 'Small groups in music lessons: creativity or cacophony?' *Research Studies in Music Education* 5.

Goehr, L. (1992) *The Imaginary Museum of Musical Works*, Oxford: Oxford University Press.

Green, L. (1990) 'The assessment of composition: style and experience' *British Journal of*

Music Education 7.3, 191–6.

Hargreaves, D. (1986) *The Developmental Psychology of Music*, Cambridge: Cambridge University Press.

Hennessey, S. (1998) 'Teaching composing in the music curriculum' in Littledyke, M. and Huxford, L. (eds), *Teaching the Primary Curriculum for Constructive Learning*, David Fulton.

Hickey, M. (1997) 'Understanding children's musical creative thinking processes through the qualitative analysis of their MIDI data' abstract in *Bulletin of the Council for Research in Music Education* 131, 29–30.

Holbrook, D. (1967a) *Children's Writing*, Cambridge: Cambridge University Press.

—— (1967b) *The Exploring Word*, Cambridge: Cambridge University Press.

Holdsworth, B. (1988) 'Marion Richardson' *Journal of Art and Design Education* 7.2, 137–54.

Hunt, F. (1999) 'Discussions with children about composers and composing' (unpublished).

Kratus, J. (1989) 'A time analysis of the compositional processes used by children ages 7–11' *Journal of Research in Music Education* 37.1, 5–20.

—— (1994) 'Relationships among children's music audiation and their compositional processes and products' *Journal of Research in Music Education* 42.2, 115–30.

Kirwan, B. (1997) 'Composing Songs at Key Stage 2' *Primary Music Today* 9, Hebden Bridge: Peacock.

Lanyon, M. (1998) 'Using Music Explorer on RM computers' *Primary Music Today* 10, Hebden Bridge: Peacock.

Loane, B. (1984) 'Thinking about Children's Compositions' *British Journal of Music Education* 1.3, 205–32

Littleton, J. D. (1991) *The Influence of Play Settings on Pre-school Children's Music and Play Behaviours*, Ph.D. Thesis: University of Texas at Austin, order no: 9128294.

Lowenfeld, V. (1939) *The Nature of Creative Activity*, London: Routledge and Kegan Paul.

McCartney, P. (1999) Interview with Michael Parkinson, *Parkinson*, BBC1 December 3.

Milton Smith, E. J. (1985) 'Art teacher training in Britain 1852–1985 with special reference to Leeds' *Journal of Art and Design Education* 4.2, 103–46.

Moog, H. (1976) *The Musical Experience of the Pre-School Child*, trans. C. Clarke, London: Schott.

Moorhead, G. E. and Pond, D. (1941) *Music of Young Children: 1 Chant*, Santa Barbara, California: Pillsbury Foundation for the Advancement of Music Education. Republished 1978.

—— (1942) *Music of Young Children: 2 General Observations*, Santa Barbara, California: Pillsbury Foundation for the Advancement of Music Education. Republished 1978.

—— (1944) *Music of Young Children: 3 Musical Notation*, Santa Barbara, California: Pillsbury Foundation for the Advancement of Music Education. Republished 1978.

Moorhead, G. E., Sandvik, F. and Wight, D. (1951) *Music of Young Children: 4 Free Use of Musical Instruments for Musical Growth*, Santa Barbara, California: Pillsbury Foundation for the Advancement of Music Education. Republished 1978.

NACCCE (National Advisory Committee on Creative and Cultural Education) (1999) *All Our Futures: Creativity, Culture and Education*, report of the NACCCE. London: Department for Education and Employment.

Nankivell, E. H. (1999a) *Group Composition: A Relevant and Practical Model for Use in the Primary School Classroom*, Unpublished M.Phil. dissertation, University of Huddersfield.

—— (1999b) *People Gathering Great Big Noises*, booklet and CD of a Performing Rights

Society Composer-in-Education Project.

Odam, G. and Paterson, A. (1999). 'The creative dream: composing in the secondary classroom' paper given at the Research in Music Education Conference, University of Exeter, England.

Paynter, J. (ed.) (1981) Schools Council Project: Music in the Secondary School Curriculum Working Paper 8, *Music in the 16+ Examination*, York: University of York.

—— (1982) *Music in the Secondary School Curriculum*, Cambridge: Cambridge University Press.

—— (1992) *Sound and Structure*, Cambridge: Cambridge University Press.

Paynter, J. and Aston, P. (1970) *Sound and Silence*, Cambridge: Cambridge University Press.

Richardson, M. (1948 posthumously) *Art and the Child*, London: University of London Press.

Perkins, G. (1998) *Composers in Education 1996–7*, a report for the Performing Right Society, London: PRS.

Pond, D. (1979) 'The roots and the creative emergence in a free environment of the young child's native musicality' address delivered 10 February 1979 at the Music Educators National Conference, Eastern Division, Atlantic City. Available from MENC historical Center, University of Maryland, Maryland 20742.

—— (1981) 'A composer's study of young children's innate musicality' *Bulletin of the Council for Research in Music Education* 68, 1–12.

Read, H. (1943) *Education Through Art*, London: Faber and Faber.

Schafer, R. M. (1975) *The Rhinoceros in the Classroom*, Canada: Universal Edition.

Serafine, M. L. (1988) *Music as Cognition*, New York: Columbia University Press.

Shehan Campbell, P. and Teicher, J. (1997) 'Themes and variations on the creative process: tales of three cultures' *Research Studies in Music Education* 8.

Shelley, S. J. (1996) 'Investigating the musical capabilities of young children' *Bulletin of the Council for Research in Music Education* 128, 26–34.

Sloboda, J. (1985) *The Musical Mind*, Oxford: Clarendon.

Small, C. (1998) *Musicking*, Hanover, N.H.: Wesleyan University Press.

Smith, G. and Walker-Smith, N. (1994) *American Originals*, London: Faber and Faber.

Smith, R. and Best, D. (1980) *The Function and Assessment of Art in Education*, Leeds: Association of Art Advisers.

Southcott, J. (1990) 'Dr Satis Coleman' *British Journal of Music Education* 7.2, 123–32.

Spencer, P. (1974) Schools Council Project: Music in the Secondary School Curriculum.

—— (1981) *The Influence of Pop on Creative Music in the Classroom*, working paper 1, York: University of York.

Sundin, B. (1998) 'Musical creativity in the first six years' in Sundin, B., McPherson, G. and Folkestad, G. (eds), *Children Composing*, Malmö: Malmö Academy of Music, Lunds University.

Sundin, B., McPherson, G. and Folkestad, G. (eds) (1998) *Children Composing*, Malmö: Malmö Academy of Music, Lunds University.

Swanwick, K. and Tillman, J. (1986) 'The sequence of musical development: a study of children's composition' *British Journal of Music Education* 3.3, 305–40.

Upitis, R. (1992) *Can I Play You My Song?* New Hampshire: Heinemann Educational.

Verney, J. (1981) 'The integrated instrumental teacher' British Journal of Music Education 8.3 245–70.

Wiggins, J. (1994) 'Children's strategies for solving compositional problems with peers' *Journal of Research in Music Education* 42.3, 232–52.

Wilson, B. (1981) 'Implications of the Pillsbury Foundation School of Santa Barbara in perspective' *Bulletin of the Council for Research in Music Education* 68, 13–25.

Winterson, J. (1994) 'An evaluation of the effects of London Sinfonietta projects on their participants' *British Journal of Music Education* 11.2, 259–70.

—— (1996) 'So what's new? A survey of the education policies of orchestras and opera companies' *British Journal of Music Education* 13.3, 129–42.

Young, S. (1995) 'Listening to the music of early childhood' *British Journal of Music Education* 12.1, 51–8.

—— (1999) 'Interpersonal features of spontaneous music-play on instruments among three and four year olds' paper given at conference on Cognitive Processes of Children Engaged in Musical Activity, University of Illinois at Urbana-Champaign, June 1999.

Young, S. and Glover, J. (1998) *Music in the Early Years*, London: Falmer Press.

Index